W9-AOQ-118

Labrador Retrievers

Joan Hustace Walker

BARRON'S

Contents

History of the Lab

The earliest origins of the Labrador Retriever are thought to have developed over a period of more than 200 years, dating back to the late 1500s in Newfoundland as an all-purpose retriever/fisherman's dog.

By the 1830s, the great sportsmen of England took a keen interest in the breed that was developing in Newfoundland and began importing St. John's Water Dogs. Within 50 years, St. John's dogs became so highly valued as hunting dogs in England that it was estimated that more than 60 gamekeepers were training, breeding, and looking after these treasured imports. It was this incredible interest in the breed by the British that made the survival of the Labrador Retriever possible.

Just as the Lab had attracted the attention of England's nobility, the Lab had also garnered followers overseas in the United States. In the 1920s, the gentlemen's sport of shooting, which had become popular in Scotland, quickly became a passion among America's wealthy. Affluent individuals with a penchant for hunting imported Labradors from famous English kennels and employed Scottish gamekeepers to develop and run their shooting preserves and sprawling hunting estates.

It wasn't long before American sportsmen—beyond those with great wealth—were attracted to the superb hunting abilities of the Labrador and gained a keen interest in the breed. From the late 1930s to the late 1970s, the Labrador Retriever grew in popularity among competitive field trialers—those seeking an excellent personal hunting dog in the field, and also in the show ring. The popularity of the breed remained in a controlled, gradual climb, which enabled breeders to retain the breed's strong hunting characteristics, health, and sound temperament.

Then, in the early 1980s, pet owners discovered just how amazing this breed could be as a family dog under the right conditions. Because the Lab was so adaptable, the "right conditions" encompassed a broad range of living conditions and family situations. It is at this point that the breed's popularity made the jump to include not only sportsmen and

5

Labs as Working Dogs

Along the way to his rise in fame, the Labrador Retriever earned kudos for his potential as a working dog outside that of a superb hunting dog in marshes and fields. The Labrador is commonly used in many service dog programs for the blind and disabled. The breed is also revered for his work in arson detection, and in some areas of the country, the Labrador is the only breed trained for this work. Additionally, the Labrador has served for decades as a scent detection dog for the Transportation Security Administration (TSA) and for some time, the TSA actually bred Labrador Retrievers specifically for explosives detection work.

Working Labs are frequently used as single-purpose, scent detection dogs in military, police, and government agency K-9 programs. As a single-purpose K-9, these dogs are not required to perform patrol dog duties (i.e., apprehending criminals), and are reserved for detection work only, trained to scent materials such as narcotics, explosives, illegal agricultural imports, or smuggled money.

Labrador Retrievers are also used quite honorably both as K-9s and as volunteers in Search and Rescue (SAR) work, and have been attributed with the finds and rescues of many missing, lost, and/or trapped individuals, as well as providing closure for families of those who are less fortunate.

women but pet owners, and those involved in performance events, search and rescue, service dog training, and K9 scent detection programs (e.g., explosives, arson, narcotics, smuggled currency, agriculture, etc.). Fortunately, the Labrador, unlike many other breeds, was able to make this huge jump in popularity without serious health and temperament problems.

A BREED WITH A PURPOSE

The Labrador Retriever was bred for the build (e.g., body type, coat length, physical endurance, etc.), as well as the characteristics (e.g., drives, temperament, etc.) to perform upland game and waterfowl hunting duties. Many of these qualities began to take shape, literally, as the St. John's dog developed: a broad chest, buoyant body, and webbed feet made for an excellent swimmer, and an efficient distribution of body fat with a thicker, shorter double coat that repelled water made the dog more resilient to Newfoundland's icy waters. The development of the Labrador's unique "otter tail," a thick, three-quarter-length, rudder-like tail that is mostly straight and held lower than most tails, produced an exceptional water-retrieving dog.

The Labrador Retriever's breeding and refinement that continued in England during the 1800s produced a gun dog that is equally qualified to hunt both on land and in water. The Lab was bred to hunt alongside an individual as a personal hunting companion, rather than to run ahead at great distances. The Lab was also bred to be calm and patient, as waiting in marshes and blinds might be required for long periods of time, yet have the endurance to hunt all day if required.

The Labrador Retriever can scent a shot bird or track a wounded bird. The breed is noted for its "soft" mouth: the ability to gently carry shot game so the meat of the bird is not damaged. The Lab is bred for tremendous courage, as it is not easy for a dog to leap into icy waters or fight his way through thick and unforgiving underbrush to retrieve fallen game. And of course, there is the Lab's incredible innate drive to *retrieve*.

All of these qualities and characteristics are so ingrained in the Labrador that even though the Lab jumped into popularity in recent decades, much of the original Lab remains uncorrupted today.

BREED COLORS

Labrador Retrievers come in three colors: black, yellow, and chocolate.

Black Labs should be solid black; however, they often have snips of white markings, particularly on the toes, pads of the paws, chest, and sometimes a spot on the chin. Anything larger than a spot on the chest, however, is a disqualification in the show ring.

Yellow Labs range in color from a very rich, almost red-fox coloring to a creamy, nearly white color. The yellow Labrador's lips, nose and eye rims should be black; however, a yellow Lab's black nose can lighten up with age and/or in colder climates. It also can get a pinkish cast to it. A yellow Lab that is *born* with a pink nose *and* has a pink or chocolate eye rim coloring is called a "Dudley," and cannot be shown in the breed ring.

Chocolate can range in color from a beautiful, deep liver color to a light, café au lait coloring. Chocolate Labradors have chocolate eye rims, lips, and noses. The chocolate color is the least recorded of the three colors of the Labrador Retriever.

Historically, the predominant—and most desirable—color among Labrador Retrievers is black, with yellow and then chocolate coming in second and third respectively. In fact, long ago there was even some bias among hunters against colors *other* than black. Not so anymore. In fact, yellow is currently edging out black as the most popular color for Labrador Retrievers. Of course, as most longtime Labrador owners will tell you, the color of the wrapper doesn't make the Lab. It's what's inside that makes the Labrador Retriever.

Unless, of course, that color is *silver*—and then, what's inside may not be 100% Lab.

Silver Is Not the New Black

A recent phenomenon occurred in the Labrador, in which a purported "rare" and exotic silver coat color, very similar to that of a Weimaraner's ghostly gray color, appeared in some Labrador Retriever lines and was marketed, sold, and even registered by the AKC. Reputable Labrador breeders became increasingly concerned that the unknowing public was being duped into believing this was 1) a purebred Labrador, 2) a "rare" color, and 3) worth a premium price.

The genetics committee of the Labrador Retriever Club, Inc. (LRC) released a statement in March 2014 that it was the opinion of the parent club of the breed (LRC) that the silver Labrador was not a purebred Labrador Retriever. The committee noted that

it could not conclusively "…prove that the silver Labrador is a product of crossbreeding the Weimaraner to a Labrador," though the committee noted that the original breeders of the silver or "blue" Labradors were also, coincidentally, involved in the Weimaraner breed. The LRC genetics committee noted that there was solid evidence in scientific literature indicating that the Labrador had never been identified as carrying what is called "the dilute gene dd," which is the gene that would be needed to create the silver or blue coloring. The committee wrote in its report that "The Weimaraner is the only known breed in which the universality of dd is a characteristic."

So, if you fall in love with a "silver" Lab puppy, be aware that 1) it's not a purebred

Lab, 2) this is not a rare color but rather it is the influence of another breed's genetics, 3) this pup is not worth more, and 4) you are not working with a quality breeder. Unfortunately, if you've already fallen in love, it may be too late to walk away but at least you knowingly are paying a premium for a high-risk, mixed-breed puppy and are not mistakenly thinking you are purchasing a well-bred Labrador.

THE LAB TODAY

The Labrador Retriever has evolved from a fisherman's working dog, to a nobleman's sporting dog, across the pond to America to be the aristocrat's choice gun dog, back to the hardworking hunting dog of *everyman*, and onto becoming the household name for a cherished pet, as well as the breed of choice for many working dog disciplines.

Is the Lab for You?

The Labrador Retriever has been the reigning champ in popularity for decades and for good reason. He was bred for centuries to work peacefully and diligently alongside his master in the field and in marshes, creating an intelligent, mindful canine companion.

The focus of this concentrated 200-year-plus breeding, of course, was specifically to create the best drives, temperaments, and characteristics for hunting with no thought given into creating the most popular dog in the 21st century.

Fortunately for pet owners, most of the characteristics that make for an exceptional personal hunting dog make for a terrific companion dog. Although there is now a wide range in the degree of intensity between each individual Labrador Retriever's abilities and drives, all Labs still possess certain innate characteristics specific to the Labrador.

What this means to the pet owner is that the Labrador may have been "out of the hunt" for a few generations, but the "hunt" is still in him. How intensely these hunting drives and characteristics remain in the dog, however, can be viewed by pet owners as benefits in some instances and as challenges in others. Knowing what the characteristics and drives of the Labrador are, and what benefits and challenges they can present to you as a pet owner, allows you to be far better equipped in predicting the impact a Labrador will have on your life and recognizing what lifestyle changes you may need to make to best live with a Lab, and ultimately, if a Labrador is really the right dog for you.

WHAT MAKES THE LABRADOR SO GREAT?

The Labrador Retriever has a tremendous amount of good qualities, which is why he is the most popular dog in the world. It's also worth noting that these qualities must be very ingrained in the breed because there are very few breeds that would have been able to survive the explosion in popularity that the Labrador did in the 1990s and still have maintained, for the most part, such steady temperaments and general good health.

Temperament The Lab is known for his good-natured, congenial, roll-with-it temperament that makes him a great personal companion, as well as a terrific family dog. He is a top pick for the novice dog owner as he does not typically "test" for leadership rights, but usually is willing to accept his place as a loyal family member.

Overall Good Health Quality Lab breeders work to keep potential health problems low by testing for inherited diseases known to be carried by some Labradors (e.g., hip dysplasia, elbow dysplasia, certain eye disorders, Centronuclear Myopathy [CNM], exercise-induced collapse [EIC], etc.) and by only breeding dogs that are clear of disease. The well-bred Lab has remained remarkably healthy considering just how popular he has become over the past 20 years even among quality breeders, and has an average life span of approximately 12 to 13 years.

Trainability The Labrador was bred to be a personal hunting companion and is uniquely in tune with his handler. He is an enthusiastic learner with the capability of intense focus at an early age. With consistency from his

13

handler, he is a joy to train, and is very forgiving of handler errors. In other words, if you make a mistake and have to retrain an exercise, the Lab, unlike other breeds, is smart enough to realize this and goes, "Oh, okay. I got it. You want me to do it *this* way now. Okay!"

Athleticism This is the dog that can hunt, swim, run, be a jogging companion, and a weekend hiking buddy. He can compete in virtually every competitive sport open to all breeds, and he is, of course, exceptional in his own areas of expertise. If you want a dog that can do it all, the Lab is a great choice.

High Tolerance The Lab is a solid dog both physically and mentally and is not easily offended by accidental bumps or tugs, making him a great companion for responsible children with sensible parents. He typically gets along great with other dogs, and doesn't normally take offense easily when playing with physical dogs, as more sensitive or reactive breeds may be prone to do.

Low Maintenance Coat It's a wash-and-wear, soak-and-shake kind of coat! The Lab's double coat *does* shed, but it's easy to take care of with regular brushing and an occasional washing. That's it. No clips, trims, or special grooming tricks to keep this fella looking fabulous.

Animal Friendly Labradors are hunting dogs, so you might think keeping a Lab with

a non-dog pet (e.g., cat, rabbit, etc.) might be problematic. But, they are retrievers: they retrieve shot game, not track it down and kill it. Therefore, it really is not in the Labrador's nature to harm anything (of course there are always exceptions). But, usually, Labs are a great choice for a multispecies home.

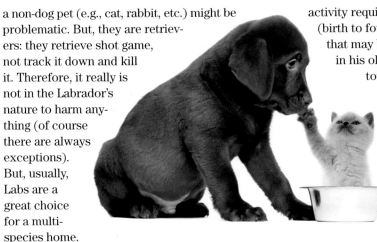

All-around Hunting Dog Whether you want to hunt upland birds or waterfowl, the Labrador (from tested hunting lines) can make a terrific personal hunting companion on the weekends, and a great family dog during the week.

IS THE LABRADOR A CHALLENGING BREED?

If a dog wasn't a little challenging, it would be sold in a toy store and filled with fluff. Labradors are living, breathing, intelligent beings and are also one of the finer hunting breeds ever created, so they do have certain unique characteristics that may make some pet owners feel that Labs have higher demands as house pets. However, Labs don't normally engage in any unusual behavior. Most behaviors, that are not desirable to the pet owner, can be easily modified with training or a few adjustments to the home or lifestyle.

High Activity Level All puppies are active. All young dogs are active. But the activity requirements of a young Lab (birth to four years)—even one that may become a hearth dog in his old age—can come as a total shock to a family. If you take a dog that was bred to go *all day* hunting and then put him in a home, what does he do? He goes *all day* in the home. *Running and running and running and…* You get the picture. Solution: The young Lab needs at least thirty minutes to an hour of serious exercise *twice* a day.

Attention Hog The Labrador Retriever was bred to work beside a hunter, looking to him throughout the day for instruction, listening at a distance for direction when retrieving, and constantly working and listening and looking. Now that hunting dog is in your home, and he's looking at you, listening, following you, bringing you his toys, and begging you to interact with him. And when you don't? Well, sometimes *any* attention to the Lab may be better than no attention at all, and the Lab may resort to misbehaving to get your attention and interaction. Solution: Exercise, train, and have fun interacting!

Mental Needs/Destructiveness The Labrador Retriever was bred to be a highly intelligent hunting dog. As a pet, this translates into a dog that needs constant mental stimulation. If the Lab doesn't have the opportunity to experience new things, travel to new places, learn new skills, detect new

15

scents, he will become bored. If this happens, most often the Lab will try to entertain himself, which usually involves digging, chewing, ripping, barking, climbing, tearing, eating, running, etc. Solution: Mentally stimulate your Lab with regular interaction through training, exercise, "jobs," and travel.

Slime Labs were bred to be retrievers and retrievers carry things in their mouths. Some Labs will *always* have something in their mouths, others maybe not so much (maybe...). Some Labs have "wetter" mouths than others, but regardless, whatever is in the Lab's mouth it will be covered in a layer of Lab slime. Solution: Remind yourself that it could be far worse; Labs have dry mouths compared to breeds with large flews, such as St. Bernards.

Chronic Health Problems When the demand far exceeds what quality breeders can produce, "other" breeders will be there to fill the need for puppies. With the Labrador Retriever's explosion in popularity, the boon of "opportunistic" Labrador Retriever breeders exploded, too. Fortunately, the breed was quite healthy at the beginning of this boom. What happened, however, was that "opportunistic" breeders—those interested in producing puppies for cash and not for hunting, show, performance, and betterment of the breed—didn't take the time and effort to test for genetic diseases, or even carefully select healthy lines from which to breed. The result was—and is still today—many poorly bred Labs with genetic diseases (See Lab Health: page 60), as well as those that seem to have lowered immune systems and are more prone to allergies and skin disorders, which are both chronic and costly, lifetime veterinary treatment situations. Solution: Invest your money and your heart wisely and purchase a well-bred puppy from a quality breeder; don't support the opportunistic breeder. Or, consider saving an adult dog through Lab Rescue (see page 25).

Training Needed Labs are tremendously fun to train; however, *they need training.* And they need training early on because training an adolescent Lab with an adult body and strength that has absolutely no manners (and is knocking kids down like bowling pins) isn't fun. Solution: Start training the Labrador puppy as soon as he sets paws into your home.

Shed/Odor The Labrador was bred to withstand icy waters and retrieve waterfowl. To do this, he needed a double coat, and a coat that produced oil so that it could shed water.

In cold climates, the double coat will shed most profusely in the spring and then again in the fall. In extreme climates, the double coat will shed year-round. With pets that spend most of the time indoors (as yours will!) expect your Lab to shed *all the time*. Then there's the oil… The Lab's coat oil keeps his coat and skin healthy; however, it can give off an odor when your dog has been very active outdoors and comes indoors, or if you haven't bathed your Lab in a very long time. Solution: Brush your Lab regularly and bathe as needed.

Poor Temperament As noted above in "Chronic Health Problems," opportunistic breeders took advantage of the demand for Labs during the popularity explosion and were breeding to meet the demands of the public with no concern for preserving the core elements of the Lab: his good health, hunting drives/character, classic conformation, and tremendous temperament. As a result, today there are some Labradors that do not have great temperaments, making them unsuitable as family dogs and too challenging for novice dog owners to successfully raise into balanced, well-adjusted, social Labs. Solution: Invest your money and your heart wisely and purchase a well-bred puppy with a fantastic temperament from a quality breeder; don't support the opportunistic breeder. When you are a more experienced Lab owner, you can help with socialization and early training by fostering puppies and young dogs in need through Lab Rescue (see "The Adoption Option," page 25).

THINKING IT THROUGH

You've balanced the qualities that make owning a Labrador Retriever so wonderful. You've also carefully considered the potential challenges that are inherent with raising a dog that was bred to be one of the world's finest hunting dogs. Now you have to ask yourself the hard question: Are you willing to be flexible enough with your lifestyle, or even make permanent changes to your lifestyle, to easily accommodate a dog?

The Labrador Retriever is able to fit well into so many homes and with so many different lifestyles because he is very adaptable. But, he is a dog and as amazing as he is, even the Labrador has his limits. So what it boils down to really is if you can make your home and life work for *him*. Can you be home for him every four hours to allow him to relieve himself during the day? Can you provide him with the vigorous exercise he will need? The mental stimulation? The human contact? If you travel often, will he be able to travel with you?

Most living situations can be accommodated if the pet owner is innovative and puts the Lab's needs first when coming up with solutions. If you are willing to make your house a home for your Lab, and you are willing to change your lifestyle to make it the lifestyle for you *and* your Lab, your Labrador will reward you with the loving depth of a relationship that you will treasure for a lifetime.

Finding the Right Companion

You've weighed the benefits and the challenges of raising and owning a Labrador Retriever, and you think this is the dog for you, now where do you find your future companion?

When choosing your puppy, the most important decision may not be *which* puppy to pick but *which* source to go to for your puppy. Finding a litter of Labrador Retrievers for sale is not hard; there are litters for sale advertised everywhere. Finding a litter of well-bred puppies—those that have been bred for the best possible health, temperament, and physical attributes possible—is much more difficult to sort out, unless you know where to look.

Can you find an adorable Lab puppy from a litter down the street that will make a fantastic lifelong companion? Yes. Absolutely.

If you are going to *buy* a puppy, you should be putting your money into the healthiest puppy possible—and that means not only healthy physically, but mentally as well. The puppy that is not bred well is much more likely to have costly chronic health issues, such as allergies and certain skin disorders, or potentially serious inherited disorders (see *Lab Health*, page 60). *This* is the puppy that you can rescue or foster and you can still pour your heart and soul into, but you should not be pouring your resources into his care *unknowingly.* The poorly bred puppy is also more likely to inherit a quirky temperament (or "learn" one from a poor environment), which is an issue that can

be difficult for even experienced owners to correct.

The puppy that you should be investing your money into is the one that a breeder has invested his or her lifetime into trying to create the healthiest, most intelligent, sociable, structurally sound Labrador possible. *That* is the puppy you want to find.

BREEDERS, BREEDERS EVERYWHERE...

So who are these elusive quality breeders who place an emphasis on health, temperament, movement and build, and produce outstanding examples of the breed? With the Labrador Retriever, you will find these breeders involved in any combination of events, and they will all be associated with the AKC, whether through show, field, hunt tests, performance events, or any combination thereof.

- **Show/Conformation:** Achieving a show championship on a Labrador is very competitive, as the numbers of outstanding dogs and good handlers are so high (and only one male dog and one female dog earn "points" toward a championship at each show). The occasional politics in the ring can also make it quite difficult and expensive to "finish" even an excellent and well-deserving dog's championship. Those breeders who persevere and show their dogs to titles have truly achieved an honor that should be recognized. For these breeders to take additional time to earn hunting titles in AKC Hunt Tests and/or Working Certifications through the LRC, is an exceptional testament to their devotion to keeping the Lab's full range of drives intact in their breeding.

- **Field Trials:** These breeders produce dogs that compete in the AKC's highly competitive field trials. The dogs are bred to be able to work incredibly challenging multiple marks, blinds, and distances and tend to be leaner in build than what is known

Quality Breeders

Quality breeders focus on producing a well-balanced Labrador Retriever.

- Health—both parents tested and certified free of genetic diseases common to the breed
- Temperament—both parents possess solid, friendly temperaments
- Correct conformation—both parents follow the breed standard closely and do not have any disqualifying points; also, if not from hunting lines, one or both parents have received conformation championship
- Potential—one or both parents have received titles/awards in hunting (field trials or hunt tests), to prove they have retained the innate qualities and drives needed for hunting

as the "English-type" or blockier type Lab. The field Lab can be a very high-drive, high energy Lab and must have a sport, exercise, or job to be happiest. Field trial Labs are not often shown for two reasons: 1) training a field trial Lab is very time consuming and trialing him is even more consuming and expensive; and 2) it takes an incredible dog to have the "run" needed for the field and still have the conformation required of a show Lab. There have been some Labs who have been able to do it all and have been crowned Dual Champions. But, it is a very rare dog that can do this.

- Hunt Tests: Breeders who participate in AKC Hunt Tests are often either those who are producing Labs as personal hunting dogs and are looking to compete with their dogs in the off season, or they are show breeders who are putting titles on their

Referrals

Keep in mind when you initiate contact with the breeder that he or she may not have a puppy or a litter available at the time. However, the breeder may be able to recommend a breeder who has a litter available. If this is the case, *contact them!*

champions to ensure that their lines continue to carry the drives and characteristics needed for a true gun dog. These breeders are good sources for personal hunting dogs and dogs for AKC Hunt Test events.

- **Working Certificates:** The LRC started a certificate program in 1931 that certifies the abilities of the Labrador and his retrieving instincts. Breeders who are active in show/conformation will often pursue working certificates for their title dogs to confirm the drives and gun dog characteristics are strong in their lines. Breeders do not "breed" for Working Certificates per se, but you will find show, hunt, and field breeders who also get Working Certificates.

- **Performance Events:** Labs typically aren't "bred" for performance events, but a breeder may have one in a litter that he or she knows will excel. If a breeder is involved in performance events, often he or she has his or her dogs handled by a professional and then competes personally with his or her dogs for additional titles (and fun). The performance Lab is athletic and highly trainable with the drive and energy to compete in a variety of competitive and non-competitive/titling sports, such as agility, flyball, obedience, rally, tracking, dock dogs, etc.

The Labrador Retriever Club, Inc. (LRC), is the parent club for the Labrador Retriever with the AKC. All Labradors that compete in AKC field trials, hunt tests, and conformation shows are registered with the AKC, so this is really the best place to begin your search for a quality breeder. The LRC has a website at: *www.thelabradorclub.com.*

From the LRC's webpage, you can navigate to the "Breeders" page, where you can search for breeders by state, city, name, kennel, or by driving distance from your zip code. Additionally, each breeder's information section includes contact information, website links, health tests information (the certifications for which the breeder routinely tests his or her dogs), colors, and the activities in which the breeder is active. Note: If you want to hunt, show, or compete in performance events, then this "Activities" listing is very important to examine.

Once you've found a potential breeder, you can expect a few things to happen. First, the breeder will want to learn a lot about you: your experience with dogs, your dog training abilities, what type of home you can provide

for the dog, your expectations for the dog, and more. In addition to talking to you on the phone and most likely having you fill out an online questionnaire, the breeder is going to want to meet you in person, as well as your spouse or significant other, and your children. The breeder will want to see the dynamics of your family as well as how you and your family members interact with the breeder's adult dogs. (Is anyone afraid of dogs? Dislikes dog hair? Not totally onboard with getting a Lab?) Meeting with you and your family will enable the breeder to not only determine if the Lab is the right breed for you but also what type of puppy will be best in your home.

CHOOSING THE RIGHT PUPPY

You've found a great breeder. The litter has arrived. Oh my goodness! There are ten precious little fuzzy Labbies! How in the world do you decide?

Since the moment these puppies were born, the quality breeder has been watching their every move. They've been weighed

daily, monitored, handled, played with, and observed. By the time the pups are ready for placement into homes, the breeder will have a very good idea of all the pups' temperaments, recognizing hunting drives, early scenting abilities, and other critical "Lab" skills, as well as who is the clown of the litter, the sassy pup, the pup that sits back and figures things out, the pup that has shown early prowess as an escape artist, the loving pup, the nonstop pup, etc., etc. In a well-bred litter, as many as six or more of the 10 pups may already have been selected by the breeder as having potential for competition, whether that is for show, hunting, trialing, or another sport. Of the remaining beautiful puppies, the breeder

will know *exactly* what type of homes those puppies need to thrive as happy Labs.

If you are lucky and have worked with a quality breeder, he or she will direct you to the puppies that will work best with your family and lifestyle. This is when working with an experienced breeder is such an added benefit.

If you haven't been able to work with a quality breeder, here are a few tips in what to look for when observing the litter. When you see the pups, watch how they interact. Is there a puppy that tends to beat up on his brothers and sisters, making them yip? If so, he's probably pushy and a bit of a bully and not the one you want for a pet. Is there one that seems to be timid or exceptionally reactive to noises and remains fearful after a sudden loud noise (and doesn't bounce right back to investigate)? Also, not desirable. When you hold a puppy, is he relatively relaxed (assuming you haven't just snatched him out of a mad play pile)? This is good. Does he wriggle hard and bite you? Not as good. Do you get lots of puppy kisses? Excellent. Does he come running over to you when you say, "Puppy, puppy, puppy!" Also, good. Do you think he's absolutely adorable? Superb.

Have you fallen in love yet? Great. Does it make a difference if the pup is male or female? Not really. If you are a pet owner, you will be altering your pet, so you really won't have to worry about issues such as intact male dogs marking in the house or intact female dogs coming in season. Are both dogs equally as loving and loyal? Yes. So, don't get as hung up on the "wrapper" (color, sex of the pup), as what's inside. The heart and soul of that little puppy is going to be your companion for many, many years. Choose wisely.

THE ADOPTION OPTION

If you already own a Labrador Retriever and want to assist in rescue efforts for less fortunate Labs across the country, or if you would rather adopt an adult Labrador that has come from unfortunate circumstances, there are many, many Labs in need of homes. The LRC maintains an up-to-date, searchable database of local and regional Labrador Rescues on their website that can serve as a starting point to help you find an adoptable Labrador.

Most Labs in Rescue are altered, up-to-date on vaccines and heartworm preventive, and have been thoroughly checked for temperament. (Aggressive Labs are not allowed into the program.) Dogs often enter Rescue as adolescents, as early as eight months of age, and through young adult (six years). But, senior citizens sadly also find their way into Rescue from time to time, too. The Labs are not without some "issues," such as digging, fence jumping, barking, etc., but these problems are *known* (as are any health problems), and with training and care, and guidance and mentoring from the Lab Rescue, these dogs should become great family members over time.

Bringing Your Puppy Home

Today is the day and you're bringing your new Labrador puppy
home! You have completely puppy-proofed your home and yard,
and you've purchased every supply your Lab baby could possibly
need. You are ready for a year of problem-free puppy raising.
That would be in a perfect world. Who are we kidding?

This chapter is all about getting your home as ready as you can, but there will always be things you can't foresee: items your puppy will put in his mouth that you never thought would be attractive to a dog, cabinets that you never dreamed your pup could open, vertical surfaces a pup shouldn't be able to scale. How well you prep your home and yard can make the difference between simply dealing with the destruction of the occasional homework assignment that was actually eaten by the pup, and the puppy that has to be rushed to the emergency veterinary clinic for ingesting a child's plastic ball.

Additionally, this chapter includes a handy checklist of items you'll need for puppy's arrival and first week, some tips on making those first few nights away from mom and the puppy pile as peaceful as possible, and a "How-to" on starting the housetraining process off on the right paw!

PUPPY-PROOFING

Is preparing for a Labrador Retriever puppy any different than puppy-proofing for any other kind of breed? In general terms, the puppy-proofing process is the same, except that because the Lab may have more *working* intelligence than other breeds and because the Lab has strong hunting instincts, he tends to get himself into a bit more trouble. He can *scent* or find things perhaps a bit better, he likes to hold things and "check things out" in his mouth, and he can be a bit busier than the average puppy.

Of course, as a little bitty guy, your eight-week-old puppy will be relatively easy to contain his first night, but it won't be long before he can get himself in trouble quickly. If you haven't prepared your home and yard for his arrival, make sure you do this as soon as possible.

PREPPING THE HOME

Starting from the floor up, make sure your home is picked up. That means making sure all coins, paper clips, toys, socks, newspapers, shoes, underwear, etc., should be picked up and put away. Yes, this is particularly hard if you have small children or a messy spouse, but think of it as a learning opportunity. Figure out a way to keep the puppy *out* of high mess areas if you can't keep these floors picked up. Action figures, balls, and socks can be major sources of choking hazards for puppies; don't risk this hazard.

Homemade Locks

An inexpensive way to "lock" cabinet doors is to use a sturdy rubber band (or two) and form a figure-8 around the round door knobs.

Cover all electrical cords, particularly lamp cords and computer wiring. Cover wiring on the floor with rugs or with light capacity cord covers (used to channel computer and office wiring) to prevent your pup from biting into a live wire. Turn off lamps when not in the room, unplug them and roll up cords so as not to tempt the puppy, or better yet, remove the puppy from the room and keep him supervised!

Remove all ant traps, rodenticides, roach traps, and other poisons from the floor—even if they are wedged behind refrigerators or cabinets. Your pup will very likely be able to get to these poisons if left unsu-pervised

for even a few minutes, and with disastrous results.

Vacuum, vacuum, vacuum. If your vacuum is picking up pills, prescription or non-pre-scription—even vitamins off the floor, you have reason for alarm. Even one pill dropped on the floor unnoticed will *not be* unnoticed by your Lab puppy, and if ingested (which is likely), will cause serious if not irreparable damage. Move all medications, vitamins, supplements, etc., behind cabinet doors and be super vigilant when taking these pills not to drop them. Do not leave them out on any surface *ever* and remember that no container is Lab-proof! As your puppy grows, he will be able to jump up and reach table and counter heights so, if he is determined, there is no chair, table, or counter that will be safe from his reach if he wants that pill container. And don't assume that he will not find that bottle of aspirin attractive. Labs investigate with their mouths. (It's a Lab thing.)

Purchase child-safe latches for lower cabinet doors and under counter drawers. Yes, without these child-safe latches your Lab puppy will be able to open all of these when he is tall enough and if he is motivated to do so. For this reason, too, you should move all cleaning products and any other harmful or potentially poisonous items out of any room in which the Lab may be spending any length of time unsupervised.

Clear your coffee tables and low tables of any knick-knacks, trinkets, keepsakes, and, snacks. This table level

is open game for the growing Lab puppy. And when the Lab hits adolescence and adulthood, it's the same height as that of the very happy Lab tail, which will make a clean sweep of your tables daily.

Secure garbage cans and trash cans. You can spend a lot of money on heavy, "dog-proof" free-standing stainless steel, locking garbage/trash cans and it's pretty much a guarantee that *someday* you will come home to a house strewn with trash and a sick Lab. You also can spend a lot of wasted time watching training videos on the Internet, or spend a ton of money with a trainer to ensure that all your Lab does is sit, stare, and drool at the garbage for hours on end and does not touch it. *Or,* you can safely put the garbage behind a door. Your choice. For your sanity and your Lab's, *make the right choice.* Put garbage and trash cans where the Lab can't get them.

Finally, there's the bathroom. If you keep cleaning supplies behind locked cabinet doors and are careful with medications (so they never fall on the floor), the only reasons you would want to keep your bathroom doors shut would be 1) to prevent toilet paper thievery (a penchant for some, not an affliction of all), and 2) to cut off access to the Lab's most convenient watering hole.

MAKING THE YARD A SAFE HAVEN

Whether you have acres of land or a small patio, you'll need to do some Lab-proofing of your pup's immediate play area in the backyard. The initial hazards are more size dependent, as your Lab puppy at eight weeks is relatively small and can get himself *into* holes and crevices that he won't be able to in another month. The hazards outdoors will

change as he grows into those that he can get himself *out of*, such as a low fence.

So, when you are surveying the dangers of your Lab's outdoor area, take a good look at what is containing him: your fence. If you have a wood fence, do you have any loose boards that need fixing? Or protruding nails that could harm the puppy or potentially get caught on his collar and strangle him? Holes that he could escape through? Gaps under the boards that need covering so that he can't crawl under? If you have a chain-link fence, have you made sure it is in good shape and has no holes, loose metal, missing poles, etc.?

Now turn your attention to the foundation of your home. Are there any critter holes that might be enticing for your pup to investigate? This could be very dangerous for him and needs to be eliminated. Is there a crawl space under your home that the pup can access? If so, block this access, otherwise you will find yourself under your home, crawling after your puppy. Also, if you have a deck off the back of your house, now is the time to make sure that the lattice work under the deck is intact—unless you want to go crawling under the deck after your pup as well.

Mow grass and clear brambles and debris as best as you can. Long grass makes it favorable for fleas to flourish in warmer months; brambles and debris can injure a pup or dog at play. When clearing, be mindful of what you use; many weed killers are highly toxic and others are more neutral only when they have completely dried. Be sure to read instructions and never put your Lab in danger.

Review your plantings and make sure you know if you have any toxic or poisonous plants in your yard. Commonly used shrubs in landscaping that are poisonous are junipers, boxwoods, azaleas, hollies, hydrangea, and yews. Poisonous vines that you'll want to pull include wisteria, nightshade, and winter jasmine. Other common garden varieties to be forewarned about include lantana, daffodil bulbs, clematis, coneflowers, and peonies. For a complete list of toxic plants, as well as what parts of the plants are toxic, see the listing at *www.aspca.org* under "Animal Poison Control Center."

Be cautious with decorative pebbles and stones. Labradors in particular are known for picking up stones and pebbles. If the pup chews these rocks, he can break his teeth—a problem for the older pup if it's an adult tooth. It can be fatal if the pup swallows the pebbles and stones (not as uncommon as you would think). Even if caught in time, it will be a costly veterinary expense, and quite possibly, a costly surgery. This does not mean you have to remove this landscaping item at this time; this is just a word of caution. Be watchful. Be prepared to make changes.

Mulch is another item that can be problematic. Cocoa mulch contains the same problematic chemicals as dark chocolate: theobromine and caffeine, which in low doses can cause mild gastrointestinal upset, and in higher doses can cause rapid heart rate, muscle tremors, seizures, and even death. Cocoa mulch can contain anywhere from 300–1200 mg of theobromine per ounce, making it potentially one of the highest concentrations of this chemical your pup could encounter. As with the pebbles and stones, the cocoa mulch is only a problem if your Lab is one of those pups that eats the mulch. Given the Lab's love of putting things in his mouth, odds are *good* that even though the manufacturer *says* only 2 percent of dogs will eat this mulch, your Lab will be in that 2 percent that gets very, very ill. Why risk it? Buy another mulch. Even then, keep an eye on your Labbie. Dogs love to chew on wood when given a chance, and this can result in intestinal blockage, splinters, or even exposure to insecticides.

SUPPLIES AND EQUIPMENT CHECKLIST

✔ **Collar** Ask your breeder to measure your pup's neck so that you can have a collar ready when you pick up your puppy. A plain, quick-release snap collar with a little growing room is a good choice. (Plan on buying at least two more collars as the pup grows.)

✔ **Tag** Have a tag made in advance with (at a minimum) your name and cell phone number engraved on it.

✔ **Leash** Purchase a lightweight, 6 ft leash with a small clip. Remember, this is an 8-week-old puppy. You don't want a heavy, brass clip banging him in the head when he's first learning that it's fun to walk on a leash!

✔ **Food** Have a minimum of a seven-day supply of the exact, same food the breeder used on hand and ready to feed.

✔ **Bowls** Purchase stainless steel, weighted, rubber edged/bottomed, "no-tip" bowls for your puppy. They are easy to clean, dishwasher safe, and are harder for pups to tip over. You may also want to purchase a collapsible, travel water bowl to keep in the car.

✔ **Crate** The crate should be large enough for the pup to stand up, turn around, and lie down. A small crate will be rapidly outgrown by the Lab puppy, so consider a sturdy wire crate with expandable partitions for the growing Lab, or an initial plastic crate to fit now, and then bigger crates as the Lab matures to full size.

✔ **Bedding** Choose something warm and snuggly and easy to wash. Do not use any bedding with stuffing (a top choking hazard) until you know whether or not your pup is likely to shred his belongings.

✔ **Toys and Chews** Choose chew toys wisely. Labs *can* be big chewers and they are definitely investigate-everything-by-mouth dogs. To make sure their toys are safe: balls should be too large to swallow, and canvas and plush toys should have no stuffing. Do not buy rawhide toys, as these can be chewed until gummy, creating a choking hazard if swallowed whole, or developing into a blockage if managing to reach the stomach. Vinyl and thin latex toys should also be avoided, as they can easily be ripped apart and swallowed, choked on, and cause blockages. Instead, look for products such as Nylabone puppy

and adult chew toys, size-appropriate Kong toys, and as the Lab puppy grows, chew toys and products labeled for big or heavy chewers, such as the Almost Indestructible Ball.

✔ **Housetraining Supplies** It's not a question of *if* your pup will have an accident but *when* and *where* (and on *who's* watch). Be ready and have your cleaning supplies on hand. (For a supply list, see "How-To: Housetrain Your Lab," pages 36–37.)

YOUR LAB'S FIRST NIGHT

Your pup is home. You've played with him. He's eaten. He's pottied. You nestle him in his crate and climb quietly into bed… and you make eye contact. He makes the most pitiful wail you've ever heard. This is going to be a long night.

Or is it?

Old school training would have you resist all urges to comfort the little guy. Because,

as the old pros would tell you, doing this would create a Lab-monster that would end up wanting to sleep (collective gasp here) in your bed for the rest of his life. OK. The latter part, the part about him wanting to sleep in your bed is true, but the part about creating a Lab-monster is not.

Here is what's going on. The puppy is used to sleeping in a pile of puppies. This keeps everybody warm. He's used to hearing heartbeats in the puppy pile. When you bring him home, he's all alone. No extra warmth. No heartbeats. So, his crying could be because he's lonely; he *misses* his littermates, mom, and breeder. Or, it could be because he's cold. He could be a little scared: he's in a new place. Or it might be as simple as he actually has to relieve himself (stress can increase his metabolism and increase the production of urine).

To ensure that you rule out all but the "have to relieve himself" as a reason for crying, here's a preparation list to help make puppy's first night as comfortable as possible for everyone.

- Use a crate. It's best not to let a little pup sleep in your bed right off the bat, simply because it's dangerous for the pup (you could roll over on him) and it's not a great start for housetraining (accidents happen when you're asleep). So, you'll want him to sleep in his crate until he is housetrained and pretty much accident free in the home.
- Put the crate close to your bed so your pup can see and hear you. Reach down and comfort him. Many owners find that making a bed on the floor next to the pup's crate that first night works wonders.
- Layer the crate with comfy, soft bedding, so he can snuggle into it for warmth. Layers of soft towels, or small washable quilts can work nicely, if they don't have stuffing.

- Wrap a hot water bottle in a towel and nestle it under some blankets in the crate to give the pup a warm spot to snuggle. It's not a perfect replacement for a pile of Lab brothers and sisters, but it's a start.
- Offer the pup a safe chew toy to help him fall asleep. The chew toy can often act like a pacifier and help the pup calm down and drift off to sleep.
- Spray D.A.P. (Dog Appeasing Pheromone) in the pup's crate. This is a synthetic version of the hormone emitted by nursing dogs and is a source of comfort for Labs of all ages.

Be prepared to take your pup out to relieve himself at least once during the night, and resign yourself to the fact that you'll probably be getting up pretty early in the morning for a while.

Labradors are generally considered to be one of the easier breeds to housetrain, as they mature physically a little more quickly than tiny toy breeds and are, by nature, exceptionally intelligent and willing to please. With a few simple rules, most Labradors can be reliably housetrained relatively easily.

1. Create clean space with a crate. From a very early age, a puppy learns to keep his bedding clean and eliminates as far away from his momma and littermates as possible. Foster this natural drive by using a crate as his "clean space" at home. The crate should be only big enough for him to stand up, turn around, and lie down. If it is any bigger, he can walk over to the corner, eliminate, and then go back to a far corner and lie down. Be aware that this means you will need to continually resize the crate so that it fits your growing Lab, or purchase a crate with an expandable panel that can grow with him.

He should be put in the crate quietly with a chew toy for naps. If he cries, he should be given an opportunity to relieve himself and returned to the crate. Your goal is to never allow him to soil or urinate in his crate. You want him to succeed. This means you need to be keenly aware of reasonable time limits in the crate.

Ideally, your pup should not spend more than 8–10 hours in a crate every 24 hours, so that's pretty much sleeping at night and a few hours during the day. The crate is primarily a place for your pup to go when he's fully eliminated and ready to rest.

2. Make reasonable time limits. Young puppies cannot "hold" as long as adolescents and adult dogs. A relatively calm puppy, or one that is sleeping, that has fully eliminated can be expected to rest comfortably for about the same amount of hours as his age in months. Even then, any kind of excitement, waking up from a nap, drinking, playing, eating, will usually be cause to relieve himself *right away* or within thirty minutes of the activity. Real control doesn't come until about six months.

3. Supervise. When your puppy isn't in his crate, which will be most of the time, supervise him carefully. Be the guru of puppy body language and know the signs of "I need to go…" (e.g., swift cessation of play, swift circling, sniffing, moving away from everyone, moving away from what he sees as his "clean" area, and of course, starting to squat). Predict when your pup will need to "go." Take him outside to his potty area to create opportunities for him to relieve himself up to every two hours as a young puppy.

4. Increase his space incrementally. It's easier to supervise your puppy if you limit the area in which he can play. Start with an exercise pen in the kitchen, or "tether" him to *you* with a lightweight leash, so you always know where he is. Eventually you can gate in a small room with a cleanable floor, such as the kitchen. Resist the temptation to trust him to be out of sight any time within the first six to nine months, or even the first year.

5. Praise good behavior. When you take your Lab to the location you've chosen for him to relieve himself, praise him quietly every time he *does* relieve himself. He's a good boy! If you find an accident inside, do nothing. No scolding. Ever. Dogs do not have accidents to spite you, and scolding will just make the dog fearful and the situation worse. If you see your puppy *start to have an accident*, you can say, "ah,ah,ah!" to try to stop the stream as you pick up your pup and rush him outside, but don't be cross with him! When he finishes outside, praise him! Then go back inside and clean up.

6. Review and revise. If your pup has an accident, go back through steps one through five to see if you can improve on something. Did you ask your pup to "hold" too long in the crate? Did you ignore warning signs? Were you not supervising? Did you allow your Lab too much space? Figure out what might have gone wrong and what you can do to make it easier for your puppy to succeed at house-training, and then try again.

If you feel you are following the house-training "rules," and are still having trouble getting your puppy to be reliably house-trained, or if your puppy was doing very well and then suddenly has a relapse, definitely bring him in for a veterinary check to rule out any underlying disease or condition that might be troubling the pup.

Shopping List
Housetraining Supplies
Crate
Exercise pen
Pee pads (optional to line crate and exercise pen)
Pet Stain Cleaner and Odor Removers Important products to have on hand that are made to be safe around pets but highly effective in breaking down components in urine and removing pet stains.
Paper towels
Dog gates These are available as pressure sensitive (temporary) and standing (movable), and metal (permanent) varieties that come in varying widths, styles, and heights. They can be very effective in blocking off rooms for the dogs but allowing passage for the humans.

Caring for Your Lab

Quality nutrition, basic home care, and good preventive veterinary care are the foundations of a solid life care program for your Labrador Retriever. It is important to keep this triad of health care maintenance together, as these are the few, really positive things in life that you *can* control for your Lab.

FEEDING THE PUPPY

The first rule in feeding the puppy is to use the same food that the breeder was using. A quality breeder will use a quality food. Even if you didn't purchase your pup from a quality source, you don't want to make a food change: The pup is used to this food and any sudden change in food will cause gastrointestinal distress.

Your eight-week-old pup will most likely be eating dry kibble, and that's a good thing to keep him on, as it is easy to prepare, stores well, and if he actually chews it, it can help keep tartar to a minimum. Although the amount he is eating will likely vary, he will be eating somewhere in the vicinity of 1/3 to 1/2 cup of kibble, three times a day. To see exactly how much he is eating, measure out a cup of dry kibble at meal time, give your pup thirty minutes to eat, and pick up the remaining kibble. Puppies will rarely overeat dry kibble (if there is no competition for their food, such as another pet). Measure the remaining kibble to approximate how much the pup ate. Do this for a few feedings. Now you will know how much to feed your pup at each meal.

As your pup grows, of course, you will need to increase this amount. You can expect to see "jumps" in food requirements at four months (when you can reduce feedings to twice a day) and at six months. At some point, you will see your pup begin to leave kibble in his bowl. Don't think that he is suddenly off his food. Actually, puppy food is very calorie rich and as he nears adulthood,

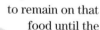

Changing Food

Changes in food should be made over a 10-day period by gradually replacing the original food with the new food.

unless he is very active or actively hunted, his calorie needs will drop and he won't need as much food. Offer him less food so he doesn't overeat, and it will be easier for him to maintain his ideal body condition. It may also be time for him to switch over to adult food.

When to make the switch is a hotly debated topic among even the best of Lab breeders. Some prefer to begin feeding the puppy adult food as early as six to nine months to prevent the Lab's bones from overgrowing his muscles. This had been a problem in the past with some puppy foods. However, there are now blends of puppy foods made specifically for medium to larger dogs, so depending on the puppy food you are feeding, it may be beneficial to remain on that food until the

pup is a year old. More of a concern may be that the pup is receiving too many calories once his metabolism begins to slow at the onset of adulthood, and he begins to pack on the pounds. Talk to your breeder and your veterinarian to discuss the issue and make the decision of when to switch to adult dog food (and to which food to switch).

FEEDING THE ADULT LAB

Obesity is perhaps the single most concerning issue with adult Labs when it comes to feeding and becomes more of an issue as the dog becomes more sedate. Athough there are always exceptions to the

rule, the Labrador is typically a good eater and finishes his dinner with gusto. As a result, he may try to convince you that he really needs more food than his body requires. And, because we often reward dogs with training treats and a snack here and there, the calories may add up faster throughout the day than we think.

Over time, obesity can compound problems with arthritis in Labradors, making joints uncomfortable sooner than from normal wear and tear, and more uncomfortable than the same arthritic joints under a lighter weight. This pain level becomes critical to his mobility when a Lab is nearing the end of his years, and it is at this time that having maintained a healthy, light weight throughout his lifetime will have played a role in extending the joint comfort and health in his senior years.

So, your first priority is not to overfeed your Labrador. To do this, make sure you understand how a healthy Lab is supposed to look: with ribs covered but detectable with light, firm finger pressure, and when viewed from above, you can see he has a discernable abdomen. Limit feeding additional snacks. If you're training a lot, calculate the training treats into the daily diet. Use kibble for treats (if the Lab is *very* food motivated), or use low-calorie training treats (some dogs love carrots).

If, on the other hand, you are working your Labrador very hard—maybe you are hunting your dog regularly or your dog has a very high activity level—you may be having difficulties keeping weight on your dog. If this is the case, talk with your breeder or your veterinarian for other food options. There are foods made specifically for sporting dogs that may better suit your dog's needs, especially during hunting season when greater demands are being placed on him.

WHAT IS GOOD NUTRITION?

A good diet needs to begin with a dog food that clearly states that it has met the nutritional requirements as established by the Association of American Feed Control Officials (AAFCO) of either "growth and reproduction" (puppies and nursing females) or "adult maintenance" (adult food). Having this certification ensures that the food not only meets the minimum nutritional requirements of the dog during that particular life cycle as determined by the AAFCO, but also (as of 2008) that the food does not *exceed* the nutritional guidelines listed for certain vitamins and minerals that have the potential to cause damage in higher concentrations, such as vitamins A, D, E, and minerals calcium, phosphorus, magnesium, and others.

A *quality* diet, however, needs to go one step further. Take a look at the nutritional adequacy statement on the pet food label and see what method the manufacturer has used to validate its claims that the food is complete and balanced. Pet food nutrition claims can be substantiated through one of three methods: formulation, feeding trial, or family.

With formulation, the nutrient content of the food is calculated by chemical analysis in the laboratory. This method does not account for either the palatability of the

food (does the dog like the taste?), or the ease of which the nutrients are digested, absorbed, and metabolized by the body. So, technically, a food could meet the AAFCO recommended guidelines, but, for example, the food may contain an indigestible form of iron in the diet. On paper, the food has the recommended percentage of iron needed for a healthy diet; however, the dog can't digest this form of iron, so the dog receives *no* iron in his diet.

The only way to test for nutrient content of the food, as well as the food's palatability, digestibility, and bioavailability, is through feeding trials. This method is more expensive for the manufacturer to conduct and it takes a longer time to produce results and analyze. However, this is really the only way to find out if the nutrients listed in the food can actually be digested and metabolized by your Lab. And, even if a food is fantastic, if a dog won't eat it, it won't do him much good, so many quality manufacturers spend a lot of research

41

and development into developing quality food that tastes good, too.

The third method you might see listed on the packaging is "family." This is a combination of formulation and feeding trial methods. The food is analyzed to prove it is a member of the manufacturer's "product family" that has already passed a feeding trial.

Quality does not come cheaply. In reality, however, you do get what you pay for: An inexpensive/low quality food needs to be fed in large amounts (large serving sizes). It produces copious amounts of stool and doesn't meet your dog's nutrient needs, possibly producing a malnourished dog, which could result in greater veterinary bills and more heartache down the road. A quality food will result in feeding less (smaller serving sizes), producing fewer stools, and providing all the nutrients your Lab needs, theoretically creating a healthier dog. At a minimum, a quality food will not have compromised your Lab's health or immune system.

FOOD CHOICES

Good nutrition comes in many forms and what type of food you pick is really up to you and your Labrador. Dog foods generally come in five forms: Dry (kibble), semi-moist (chewy/kibble), wet (canned), fresh (refrigerated), raw (frozen), homemade (cooked). Each have their benefits and drawbacks.

Dry foods: Kibble is easier to store, has a longer shelf life, and the kibble can have some teeth cleaning abilities if the Lab actually chews the food (and doesn't swallow it whole). Formulas can be age specific, breed specific, activity-level specific, grain-free, made of unique proteins (for dogs with allergies), and also in veterinary prescribed, prescription formulas.

Semi-moist foods: Typically these are highly palatable, but with no teeth cleaning benefits, and tend to have a shorter shelf life. They may also cost more than a dry kibble.

Wet/canned foods: Canned foods are very palatable and digestible but tend to be the most expensive to feed and have no teeth cleaning benefits. These foods can be very healthy, and they can also be used as topper on dry foods to encourage a picky eater. Storage of opened cans requires refrigeration, and cleanup of bowls is necessary after mealtime.

Fresh/wet (refrigerated): These foods are highly palatable, but tend to be more expensive to feed as an only source of food. They can be used to mix with a kibble.

As a food, they require refrigeration during shipping and storage.

Frozen/raw diets: Highly palatable, raw food diets can be very healthy alternative diets for dogs; however, they are not without risks for both dog and owner. In a recent study performed by the FDA Center for Veterinary Medicine (CVM), samples from commercially available raw pet food, as well as dry dog food and semi-moist dog food were tested. According to the study's results, CVM identified a potential health risk for not only the pets eating the raw food, but for the owners handling the product as well: Owners who feed their pet a raw diet may have a higher risk of getting infected with Salmonella and Listeria Monocytogenes. (In the test, 7.7 percent of the raw commercial pet food samples tested positive for *Salmonella*, and 16 percent of the raw commercial pet food samples tested positive for *Listeria monocytogenes*, compared to *no* samples testing positive with jerky-type treats including pig ears, semi-moist dog food, and dry dog food). Before embarking on a raw food diet—whether commercially prepared or home-prepared—consult with your veterinarian.

Homemade cooked: As you might expect, these diets can be amazingly healthy, and exceptionally palatable *if the diet is written by a veterinary nutritionist and followed to the letter and ounce.* These diets require precise measuring and, unfortunately, are a key source of malnourishment because owners typically start to make substitutions when one source of protein is unavailable at the grocery store, or they stop adding a

necessary supplement when their supply runs out. Measurements must be precise. Every ingredient not only counts but balances another ingredient, and these diets do require the addition of vitamins, minerals, and supplements, which can be expensive.

Supplements: Ask your veterinarian before adding any additions to your dog's food. Be sure to tell your veterinarian everything your Lab is currently receiving, from daily food to snacks and training treats. Typically, if you are feeding a quality food, your Lab will be receiving all the nutrients he will need and then some, so supplementation will not be necessary. There is a danger in receiving too much of some nutrients, which is why the AAFCO set maximum limits on certain vitamins and minerals to the feeding recommendations. So adding vitamins to your dog's diet can be potentially harmful. Again, discuss any thoughts on supplementing your dog's diet with your veterinarian.

GROOMING THE LAB FROM HEAD TO PAWS

Fortunately, the Labrador is an easy keeper, so grooming is fairly minimal. Shedding, however, can be a constant battle as the pet Labrador is mostly kept indoors, meaning his climate is "temperate." Translated: he will shed year-round. He will shed a bit more in the spring, and he will have a fall shed, but you can expect coat shed in your home throughout the year. How *much* shed depends on how full his double coat is, how much time he spends outdoors, how far north or south you live, and many other factors. But, rest assured, he will shed from a little every day to a lot every day.

The best way to stay on top of coat shed is with daily brushing and a good bath once a month during heavy shedding season, and regular brushing (two to three times a week) and bathing as needed throughout the rest of the year.

Brushing

To make sure that you brush the Lab's entire double coat (both the coarse outer coat and the downy undercoat), you'll want to use what is called a pin brush, which has rounded metal pins. Brushing your Lab's coat daily, even if he doesn't "need" it, will help to spread healthy skin oils through his coat and invigorate the skin, helping with circulation. It's also a pleasant experience for your Lab and is a great time for bonding.

During shedding season, you'll want to add some time with a shedding blade, which will help to pull shed hair that is caught under the outer coat. A specialty shedding product,

Seasonal Shedding

During heavy seasonal shedding, be sure to brush outdoors–you will be amazed at how much hair will come out with the shedding blade. And if you don't want to be cleaning Labrador hair out of your bathtub for hours, bathe your dog at a commercial self-serve dog wash. This is usually inexpensive and well worth it!

such as the FURminator, can also be very helpful in pulling out dead, shed coat quickly. Plan on following up this grooming session with a bath to remove any remaining shed coat and dead skin.

Bathing

Labrador Retrievers have wonderful, double coats that are resilient to water, which makes bathing just a little challenging—only in the initial stages of getting the coat actually wet. Water runs off the Lab about as well as water runs off a duck.

Use warm water on your Lab puppy (and adult) when wetting him down for a bath. (No cold water or outdoor hoses. You don't need to test your Lab's courage at bath time!) Wet his coat thoroughly while in the bathtub, though a little pup can be in a utility sink.

Work a small amount of dog shampoo into the coat. Make sure to wash all areas of the pup and avoid the eyes. Rinse until all traces of shampoo are gone. Then rinse again. Even a small amount of shampoo left in the coat can cause irritation. Be vigilant in washing

45

the bottom of the tub and make sure to wash the bottom of your Lab's paws one more time.

Towel him off and prepare yourself for the big shake and the crazy-wet-dog run. When you catch him again, clean his ears and trim his nails.

Ears

Inspect your Lab's ears on a regular basis for inflammation, redness, warmth, offensive smells, or a dark or reddish wax. Also, look for behavioral changes around his ears, such as head shaking, scratching, or rubbing. These could all be signs of an ear infection and/or something trapped in his ear. If your Lab is outdoors a lot, he will be more prone to coming in contact with foreign bodies and contaminated water, so it's good to start checking his ears when they're healthy so you can spot when something is amiss.

Acclimate your puppy to lying in your lap and check his ears, one at a time. Part of your routine should be to gently wipe the inside of his ears with a cotton ball lightly soaked in ear wash (your veterinarian will have good suggestions for this) and gently clean the ear leather around the ear canal. With a fresh cotton ball soaked in ear wash, wiggle the cotton ball in the ear canal and work out any excess wax. If you notice any buildup, if there is a smell, if the contact is bothering the pup, see your veterinarian.

Nails

Toenails are usually easiest to clip when they have been softened after a bath. Of course, you'll want to trim your Lab's nails far more frequently than you bathe him—usually nail trims should be every month. If your Lab has clear nails, you're lucky. You can see what you're doing. To make a clip, hold the nail so you can see the quick (the blood supply of the nail) and using the clippers, make the cut into the clear nail just past the pink. Easy, unless you have a wriggling, wild puppy in your arms, or if the nail is black (see instructions below).

To help settle a wild puppy, work on the following skills daily. With your pup sitting next to you, practice touching the clipper to his toenails *without making a clip on the nails.* Reward him with a small treat and calm praise after each tap for good behavior. Keep practicing this until he starts to tolerate one paw of toenail tapping. Then two paws. Then trim a nail. Then tap. Keep going. Keep calm and clip on.

Black nails… you can't see where the quick ends, but you can feel and see where it structurally ends. If you look at the nail from the underside, you will see an oval shape from the pad of the paw on the nail extending toward the tip. Where this oval shape ends is where the quick ends. If you feel this with your finger, you can put your finger over it and then clip just past it with the clippers.

Have on hand a product to treat a quicked toenail. Usually, this is a powder that you can dip the bleeding toenail in to help stop the bleeding. A quicked toenail bleeds profusely and it does hurt the dog. Your reaction should be that of calmness, so that you don't add alarm to the situation, however. Keep the dog calm, too, and don't let him run through the house as he will reopen the quick and bloody everything he touches. Treat the toenail and put the pup in a crate with a chew for about 20 minutes until the bleeding stops.

Teeth

Keeping your Lab's teeth and gums healthy cannot be overstressed. Use a finger brush twice a week with dog toothpaste and scrub the outside of your pup's teeth and his gums. Be sure to use dog toothpaste, as human toothpaste contains chemicals that are harmful if swallowed: Labs are talented *but no dog can spit.*

Work up to brushing your dog's teeth with a toothbrush and do this regularly. Your work will pay off as your dog ages. Healthy gums and teeth are critical for the young Lab as well as for an aging Lab's health.

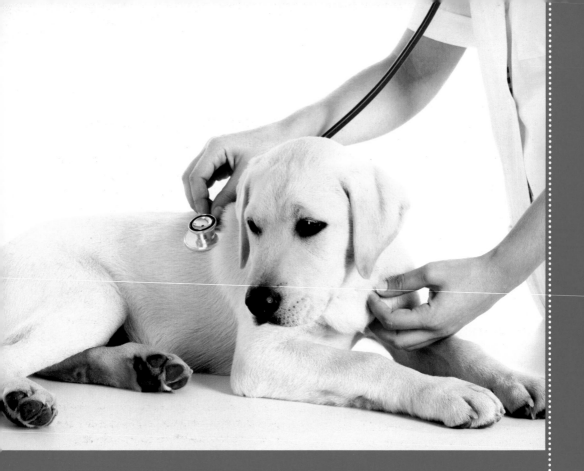

Puppy's First Exam

You are providing your Labrador with two of the
three pillars of health: quality nutrition and good
home care. The third pillar of long-term health for
your Lab is a good, preventive veterinary care.

Your Lab's preventive veterinary care should begin with your puppy's first veterinary exam where you will be setting the baseline for a lifetime of healthy, preventive veterinary care. Here, he will receive a comprehensive physical and start his vaccination series. Additionally, his preventive care program will include choosing a heartworm preventive and a plan for preventing or limiting contact with additional parasites and protozoa. As warmer weather approaches, your veterinarian will discuss the addition of flea and tick preventives. Your veterinarian will discuss the best timing for spay/neuter for your Lab puppy, as well as options for permanent identification.

THE PHYSICAL

At your pup's first veterinary appointment, which should be scheduled within the first day or two upon your Lab's arrival home, your veterinarian will give your puppy his first basic physical. You will be asked to bring a stool sample, so be sure to be prepared to do this and have this with you. This sample will be examined for worms (see "Parasites: The Ins and Outs," page 53). Your pup will have his temperature checked rectally. A dog's normal temperature is between 100.5 and 102.5 Fahrenheit.

While in the under-the-tail region, your veterinarian will make sure there are no signs of tapeworms or intestinal distress and check your pup's anal glands. From here, your veterinarian will examine your pup's skin and coat, looking for signs of unwanted fleas (flea "dirt" and flea bites), ticks, mites, lumps, bumps, signs of infections, or skin irritation.

Taking Your Lab's Temperature

Clean a digital thermometer with rubbing alcohol. Apply a small amount of petroleum jelly on the end of the thermometer. With your Lab standing, and one arm securely holding him around the hind end, and a person securely holding him at the front end, grasp the thermometer so no more than 1" of the meter will enter the pup's rectum. Holding his tail up, gently slide the meter in and hold until the thermometer beeps that the temperature has registered. Wash thoroughly in warm, soapy water and mark clearly that this is the "DOG" thermometer.

Be sure to have your veterinarian help you the first time you try to check your puppy's temperature so you do this safely.

Your Lab will have his joints and spine examined, with the veterinarian looking for any signs of soreness or tenderness. The veterinarian will palpate your pup's abdomen, looking for signs of pain, enlarged organs, lumps or tightness, and rub down through other areas of the pup's body, checking for overall weight and muscle tone, making sure no lymph nodes are enlarged, which could be a sign of infection or disease.

The veterinarian will listen to the pup's heart for heart murmurs or irregular beats and make sure your pup's lungs sound clear. Ears are examined for signs of abnormalities, infection, and ear mites (see page 57). Your Lab's eyes will be examined for signs of early disease.

Your pup's teeth will be checked, too. Your veterinarian will be tracking how the teeth are coming in and making sure there aren't any issues with the direction or position of the teeth, or size of the jaws, that could present problems as the milk teeth fall out and the adult teeth move in.

Hopefully, everything is fine and it's time for puppy vaccinations!

VACCINATIONS

Depending on your breeder, your puppy may or may not have had his first puppy vaccinations. The "core" vaccinations, or those that are considered necessary for a puppy's health, are vaccinations to protect against infection from Distemper, Adenovirus Type 2, and Parvovirus. A fourth vaccine that is generally recommended to be included in the puppy's vaccination "bundle" is the vaccination that protects against the Parainfluenza virus. Depending on your area and the risk of disease, your veterinarian will administer the combined vaccine as *either* DA$_2$P (Distemper, Adenovirus Type 2, Parvovirus) or DA$_2$PP (Distemper, Adenovirus Type 2, Parvovirus, Parainfluenza virus). Regardless of which vaccine combination is chosen, the initial vaccination in the puppy series is given between 6 and 8 weeks of age. After this initial dosage, the combined vaccine is repeated every three to four weeks through the age of 16 weeks. After the puppy series has been completed, a "booster" vaccine is given of the combined vaccine when the puppy is twelve months old, and then every three years afterward.

How serious are these viruses? Puppy owners are asked to *carry* their unvaccinated puppies into the veterinarian's office and not set them on any surfaces until they are

in the exam room, just so that the puppy isn't accidently exposed to one of these viruses. Breeders will ask prospective puppy buyers to take off their shoes before entering the house when looking at puppies, so as not to accidently carry in one of the viruses. Training clubs will not take puppies into their classes until the owners can show proof of vaccination. You will not be able to board your puppy *anywhere* until he is fully vaccinated. *That's how serious these diseases are.*

Don't risk exposing your puppy unnecessarily during the vaccination period either.

The purpose for multiple doses is that the veterinarian is trying to find the time when the puppy's mother's natural antibodies against the diseases are no longer protecting the puppy, and the vaccine is able to cause the puppy's body to produce his own antibodies. No one knows exactly when that moment is, so therefore, the puppy receives multiple injections, hoping that one or more is given when the puppy is able to make his own antibodies (and before he has been exposed to the disease).

So, don't take your pup to walk the floors at large pet stores or mega building supply stores. Avoid walking in parks with lots of dogs—you will have a lifetime to do this. Wait until he's vaccinated. There's plenty of places to take him that will be safer right now.

Another core vaccine that your puppy will receive, but that is not in the bundled vaccines, is a rabies vaccine. The rabies vaccine is given between the ages of twelve to sixteen weeks, with a booster given at one year. Then, depending on local laws in your area, your Lab will need to receive a rabies vaccination every one to three years.

NON-CORE VACCINES

In addition to core vaccines, there are also vaccines that may be recommended to you by your veterinarian if the risks are high enough

for your dog to contract this disease that they outweigh any risks that the vaccine itself might present.

The Bordetella vaccine is one that is often recommended if your Lab will be around large numbers of dogs, such as in a show or training situation. Proof of having a "current" dose of this vaccine is also required by most boarding kennels.

The Leptospirosis vaccine is a non-core vaccine that is associated with vaccine reactions and it is not effective against all strains of the Leptospira bacteria. Dogs may come in contact with strains of Leptospira bacteria that frequent heavily wooded areas, swim in lakes or ponds, or live or walk near dairy farms. The Labrador Retriever has been identified by the AKC Canine Health Foundation as one of three breeds identified to be at greatest risk to be infected by this disease, along with the English Setter and the Portuguese Water Dog.

And finally, a third non-core vaccination that your veterinarian may recommend is for Lyme disease. This vaccination is for the prevention of the most common tick transmitted disease in the world. The most common clinical symptom of the disease is lameness due to joint inflammation with lack of appetite and depression; however, Labrador Retrievers appear to be more at risk to suffer from kidney disease as a result of Lyme disease than other breeds of dogs. Whether your veterinarian recommends that you use traditional methods to protect your Lab from ticks (see below) or that your Lab is vaccinated for Lyme disease will be based on your Lab's risk of exposure to the vector tick (deer tick).

PARASITES: THE INS AND OUTS

Heartworm Preventives

Heartworm, spread by infected mosquitos, is a serious disease that is found pretty much everywhere in the United States. Depending on how badly infected a dog is and for how long (heartworm infection is usually not detected until it is quite advanced and organs have begun failing), a heartworm infection can range anywhere from seriously debilitating and painful to fatal. Heartworms damage the dog's heart, lungs, liver, and kidneys.

Infective larvae of the heartworm are injected into the bloodstream of the dog when an infected mosquito bites the dog. The Lab's double coat *does not* protect him from heartworm; he is just as susceptible as a thinner coated dog. In fact, he may be *more* susceptible as he is often outside more of his life participating in outdoorsy activities.

As the heartworm larvae mature, they travel through the dog's bloodstream and move to the heart and pulmonary arteries where they grow to maturity, all in a matter of two to three months. Maturity for a heart worm is 6 to 14 inches (15 to 36 cm) long for a female worm. A heavy infestation can be up to 300 mature worms. If caught early enough, one of the methods that has had good success

53

in treating the infestation is with a drug that contains arsenic. You can see why your veterinarian wants you to start a simple, monthly preventive immediately.

At your puppy's first appointment, you will start off with a puppy dose of heartworm preventive. Heartworm preventives are prescribed by weight, and obviously, your puppy is not going to remain at his current 12 to 16 pounds (5 to 7 kg). In fact, he is going to grow quite quickly. Your Lab will be weighed at each puppy visit to make sure he is on the correct dosage of heartworm medication, and it will be adjusted as his weight increases.

Additionally, your Lab will need to receive a yearly blood test to check for the presence of microfilariae or young heartworms. These will only be present if you missed a dose of heartworm preventive, but the annual blood test is required by all veterinarians before they can prescribe your next year's dosage.

When discussing what type of heartworm preventive to use with your Lab, be sure to discuss recent studies on side effects. Every year, new products come on the market with different combinations of heartworm/intestinal worm/flea preventive combinations. Some of these have proven to be excellent products; others have caused alleged allergic reactions and/or seizures in dogs, and others have been removed from the market. Some of the favorite products that caused seemingly no side effects are now in new combinations. Most are oral products, though a topical product was made to include tick prevention in the mix, and at one time there was an injection available. As you can see, this is a very fluid market. Your veterinarian will be the most knowledgeable source to discuss what is available on the market, what he or she believes to be the safest, and what is the most cost effective preventive to use for your Lab.

Flea and Tick Vigilance

Fleas and ticks are the bane of every dog, more so to an outdoorsy dog. There's no escaping coming in contact with them. Some of the heartworm preventives *include* a flea preventive. If your dog's heartworm preventive has a flea preventive, you may find that it's just not quite enough during peak flea season. Or, you may find that it kills a specific life

How to Remove a Tick

Part of your tick prevention program should be checking for ticks daily. Use your hands to feel every inch of your Lab and feel for bumps. It will be hard to spot tiny ticks on a black Lab. You will need to feel for them. When you find one, use tweezers and firmly grab the tick as close as possible to the dog's skin and slowly pull the tick out. If you pull too quickly and the head remains in the dog's skin, you can try to tweeze it out. Otherwise, it will naturally create a slight pimple and you can soak it out. Or, take your Lab to the veterinarian for additional assistance. If the tick is a deer tick, many owners bag the tick and take it to their veterinarians to determine if the tick was carrying Lyme disease. Consult with your veterinarian.

Ticks Can Cause

- Lyme disease—transmitted by the bite of a deer tick. This disease is definitely on the rise. Labrador Retrievers are one of a handful of breeds listed that are disproportionately suffering from one of the more fatal symptoms associated with the disease: kidney dysfunction.
- Bartonella—bacterial parasites that can be transmitted not only through a flea bite, but through a tick bite as well
- Erlichiosis—a bacterial infection that attacks the white blood cells and requires aggressive antibiotic treatment
- Rickettsia infection—in addition to the flea, which carries a form of this bacteria, different ticks carry different strains of this bacterial infection, including Rocky Mountain spotted fever, and cause different ailments
- Meningoencephalitis—a bacterial infection that can be transmitted by a tick bite, infecting the brain and spinal cord with rapid onset. It can be fatal without treatment of antibiotics.

at the time of publication that includes a flea and tick preventive; however, as noted above, this is a fluid market, so it may or may not be available at the current time.

Regardless, you are going to need a good tick preventive and likely a secondary flea product. A topical, combined, monthly flea and tick product is a good place to start. Many of the products that are available over the counter today are reasonably priced and used to be prescription products. Before using any products on your puppy, *check with your veterinarian first*. Some of these products can only be used on older puppies (e.g., 3 months, 6 months, etc.). And always pay attention to the *weight* requirements of the product. Do not use a product meant for a dog weighing 50 to 100 pounds (23 to 45 kg) on a 35 pound (16 kg) dog. You will have a very sick dog. These products are labeled for monthly use. However, many owners feel that repeated submersion in water affects the efficacy of the products.

cycle of the flea (for example, eggs and larvae) but not the adult flea. So, your Lab could still be bitten by a flea and could still get an allergic reaction to a flea. There is one topical heartworm preventive product on the market

Fleas Can Cause

- Parasitic dermatitis–an allergic reaction to flea saliva, causing hair loss and infection.
- Tapeworm infestations–ingesting fleas while trying to rid himself of the itch, a dog can ingest the source of a tapeworm infection.
- Bartonella infection–a bacterial infection transmitted by ingesting fleas, or by flea bite or scratching. Symptoms can range from an infection to severe disease and sudden death.
- Rickettsia infection–flea-borne spotted fever emerged as a disease in humans in the 1990s, and in dogs it causes vomiting, diarrhea, and fatigue.

If more protection is needed, your veterinarian may recommend a flea/tick dip or shampoo. This is a medicated dip that will kill adult fleas and ticks and will repel mosquitoes. It can only be used on pups twelve weeks or older, but it can be used weekly in severe cases. Shampoos are available that are a little less strong than the dips.

And finally, there is the flea and/or tick collar. Be sure to consult with your veterinarian before making an over-the-counter purchase, as combining the flea and/or tick collar with a topical flea and tick preventive can be dangerous to your dog. Flea and tick collars also have minimum age *and* weight requirements. Keep in mind that all of these products contain chemicals that can be harmful to your Lab and that the combination of oral, topical, dips, and collars can add up to a deadly combination. It cannot be stressed enough that to come up with an effective and safe flea and tick preventive program, *consult with your veterinarian.*

Mites

There are three types of mites to be aware of. *Otodectes cynotis*, or ear mites, are found, as you might imagine, in the Lab's ears. You'll notice your Lab shaking his head, scratching, itching, and generally being very bothered by the situation. The head shaking can become so violent that it can actually create hematomas on the tips of his ears, which when they burst, bleed *everywhere*. This type of mite is highly contagious and can pass between dogs and to other parts of the body. Treatment usually involves a commercial ear cleaner formulated specifically for mites, and an ear mite parasiticide that is used for seven to ten days and then repeated about two weeks later.

The other type of mite is *demodex canis* and is found in the pores of the skin, usually in young puppies. It typically only becomes a problem if the Lab's immune system is compromised, which could happen if the puppy comes from a rescue or shelter situation and has experienced high levels of stress, disease, poor diet, etc. Demodectic mange appears as a thinning of hair around the pup's eyes, mouth, and front legs. This type of mange can clear up on its own with a positive change in the pup's health and living circumstances and with good veterinary care, but a veterinary examination is a must.

Scabies, or Sarcoptic mange, is caused by mites and is also contagious to humans. The mites involved with this infection cause intense itching and irritation, which quickly results in horrendous infected sores and hair loss. Sarcoptic mange can be successfully treated. Therapy usually takes four to six weeks. Quarantining the pet during this time is often advised because scabies is highly contagious.

Intestinal Worms

There are roundworms, hookworms, tapeworms, and whipworms. What do you need to know? Your Lab's annual fecal exam will test for all of these worms, and depending on which heartworm preventive you use, you will have some protection against some of these worms. If your Lab tests positive for any of these worms, he will be treated and then required to provide a follow-up stool sample to ensure he is clear of worms.

- **Hookworms:** An infestation of this worm can be fatal in puppies. A puppy can become infected from his mother's milk, contaminated water, or by ingesting contaminated matter.
- **Tapeworm:** Parents be forewarned—humans can be a host to this worm, typically children. Your Lab will usually become infected by ingesting fleas with tapeworm eggs, or by ingesting transmitters such as rabbits and birds.
- **Whipworms:** Labs can become infected by ingesting infected matter (food, water,

flesh). Whipworms are difficult to eradicate as they can live in an environment (i.e., your yard) for months to years.

- **Roundworm:** Virtually all pups will be wormed for roundworms. The reason for this is that if the mother has ever been infected with roundworms, traditional wormers only kill adult worms; they do not kill encysted larvae. Years later, these larvae can migrate to the uterus to infect the unborn pups. Or, if the larvae have excysted, they can migrate in the nursing mother to the mammary gland and the puppies can be infected through the mother's milk.

Protozoa

Many people who own dogs will never have to worry about protozoa but you own a *Labrador Retriever*, so you need to be aware that there are several types of protozoa that could cause your dog issues. Why? Because it's more likely that your dog is going to be running through wooded areas, splashing through creeks, streams, ponds, rivers, and lakes and will have a greater likelihood of being exposed to certain types of protozoa, in particular, *Giardia*.

The onset of *Giardia* can be particularly hard and fast with small puppies. There's no preventive for *Giardia;* you just need to be aware of the symptoms and know that this requires an immediate trip to the veterinarian. Be on the lookout for sudden onset of diarrhea with watery and sometimes bloody, phlegmy stools. The puppy may also vomit. *Giardia* requires immediate veterinary care, good cleanup, and patient care hygiene as it can be transmitted to humans, too.

SPAY/NEUTER

At your pup's first exam, your veterinarian will also discuss what your plans are for the puppy and at what age he or she recommends spaying or neutering your Lab. For females, this is usually before the first heat cycle. For males, typically the recommendation is before seven months, prior to the male reaching maturity and marking his territory. Discuss with your veterinarian what the most current veterinary research indicates as the optimum timing for spay/neuter for your Lab puppy and have the surgery scheduled. Spay/neuter is no longer the high risk surgery it used to be decades ago for female dogs, and it is an even quicker recovery today for male dogs. You will still be able to participate in all sports, except conformation (shows).

PERMANENT IDENTIFICATION

And finally, your veterinarian will discuss with you forms of permanent identification. Dog tags should always be worn on the Lab's collar. However, dog tags can fall off. In this instance, you'll want a permanent form of identification to ensure your Lab makes it home if lost. You have two choices: a tattoo or a microchip.

Tattoo: A tattoo can be applied to the puppy, usually when he has reached near full size (for legibility reasons), under anesthesia on the inner thigh. A registration number is good to use and relatively easy to look up but sometimes a tattoo can be difficult to spot on a hairy Lab, or people don't know to look.

Microchip: A microchip is a form of radio frequency identification and requires a

scanner to read the information. The microchip is implanted between the dog's shoulder blades and though the procedure is uncomfortable, anesthesia is not required. The drawback to a microchip is that it does not provide a visible means for a rescuer to know the dog has identification. It is standard practice, however, for shelters to look for microchips.

Regardless of which method you choose, it is always wise to have dog tags *and* a permanent form of identification for your Lab, just in case.

Lab Health

The Labrador Retriever is a healthy breed. This discussion of diseases, conditions, and injuries common to the Labrador Retriever is not meant to scare you. It is meant to give you an idea of what types of issues are more common in Labs than in other breeds.

Knowing what the general symptoms are for these diseases, conditions, and injuries will give you a good general knowledge on what you might see in your Lab, and what symptoms you might keep an eye out for in the future.

SKIN

Atopic Allergic Dermatitis More than 15 percent of Labs suffer from atopic allergic dermatitis: itchy, inflamed skin caused by allergies, such as an airborne allergy (mold, dust) that falls to the floor and the dog ultimately ingests by licking his paws, or a food allergy.

Contact Dermatitis This is typically a "contact" allergy to a substance such as wool, nylon carpet, a disinfectant used on the floor, etc. Though the Lab has a double coat, he often gets contact dermatitis, or inflamed skin, in areas such as the abdomen, groin, or feet where there's little hair.

Hot Spot, Summer Sore, Moist Eczema This bacterial skin infection can have a variety of causes, but often on the Lab it stems from an ear infection or an inhaled allergen. Most often occurring in the summer months, a hot spot appears as a large, moist raw skin patch that spreads into surrounding tissues quickly.

Pyoderma This is a bacterial infection of the skin that can occur in any breed but seems to be more common in Labs, most likely because they are a breed that tends to form pressure calluses (see below). This infection causes a wet, painful area of skin with ringlike sores.

Lick granuloma If a Lab starts licking his paws, legs, or other areas of the body until it is hairless, he can create a large, ugly sore. The reason for the licking can be allergy related (itchiness) or it can be anxiety related. In the latter case, it is thought that the action of licking can release endorphins and the Lab can become "hooked" on the behavior, making this a difficult behavior to eliminate.

Pressure Calluses These are usually painless, thickened, wrinkled leathery looking patches of hairless skin over the bony pressure points of a Lab's elbows. They often are seen in older Labs that lie on hard surfaces for long periods of time.

Lipomas As the Labrador ages, he is very likely to develop fatty tumors, or lipomas, under the skin. These are benign and generally never removed unless they become large enough to cause discomfort. Lipomas *are* tested to make sure they are fatty tumors; however, if you spot any subsequent ones, make sure to have them tested to rule out something more serious.

MUSCULOSKELETAL

Arthritis Technically, arthritis is inflammation of the joints, and osteoarthritis is chronic joint inflammation caused by deterioration of joint cartilage, of which older Labs are at the greatest risk. Joint cartilage wears out over time, and osteoarthritis will become an issue that most Lab owners will have to treat eventually in their aging Labs.

Cruciate ligament rupture Labrador retrievers have a higher incidence of this

rupture, which is the equivalent of a torn knee ligament. The rupture causes partial to complete instability of the stifle joint in the rear leg and is a major cause of degenerative joint disease.

Hip dysplasia Labrador retrievers continue to be a top breed affected by hip dysplasia. Hip dysplasia in very basic terms begins with an ill-fitting hip joint. The ball of the femur is loose in the pelvic socket and this laxity causes a constant cycle of grating, fracturing, rough healing, more grating, fracturing, more rough healing, etc., causing gross disfiguration of both the ball of the femur and the pelvic socket. This results in poor motion, excruciating pain, and inflammation. Weight management and medical therapies can help with less serious cases of hip dysplasia; surgery can be successful for more serious cases, albeit expensive.

Elbow dysplasia Elbow dysplasia causes lameness in the foreleg. Symptoms are usually seen when the Lab is between four to ten months old and include forelimb lameness, stiffness, and pain. Surgery can have a fair to good prognosis but is, again, expensive.

Osteochondritis dissecans (OCD) Excessive cartilage and deficient bone growth in the Labrador's shoulder causes a severe lameness condition that is referred to as OCD or "shoulder dysplasia." The cause is unknown but is thought to be genetically based. Surgery can provide a range of results from "restricted" to "excellent."

Achondroplasia This is a form of OCD in which the forelimbs do not grow to normal size, resulting in dwarfism. Though much rarer in Labs than OCD, achondroplasia does occur and has been linked with an eye abnormality called *focal retinal dysplasia*, which occurs when small folds appear within the retinal tissue and cause blind spots in the dog's vision.

Muscular dystrophy This inherited, degenerative disease causes muscle wasting and abnormal gait. It is found in the Labrador (primarily in newborn puppies) and is caused by the deficiency of a muscle membrane protein called dystrophin. There is no cure for this devastating disease, and at this point, no known treatments are effective.

Cold Water Tail This is a unique condition in which a Lab's tail appears to be broken, and hangs limply from the tail base or may be held out three to four inches from the tail base and *then* hangs limply. Its exact cause is not known. Researchers believe that there is a similarity between cold water tail and a condition in humans called "delayed onset muscle soreness," which is caused by over-conditioning. Seasoned dog trainers feel that anti-inflammatories are helpful in improving the recovery time for regaining tail movement, but no studies have been performed to confirm this.

Hereditary Myopathy Also known as hereditary muscle disease or non-inflammatory myopathy, this disease occurs when muscle fibers stop functioning, resulting in muscular weakness. It is seen specifically in Labradors, particularly in yellow Labs. Symptoms seem to appear between the ages of three and four months and include abnormal joint position, gait, muscle weakness, an arched back, an odd downward flexion of the pup's head and neck, and even sudden collapse. Treatment is directed at easing symptoms, as there is no known cure, though clinical signs of the disease seem to stabilize when the dog reaches twelve months of age.

EYE DISORDERS

Cataracts Labrador Retrievers can suffer from many forms of cataracts, some of which are relatively harmless; whereas, others are

more aggressive. In some cases, eyesight can be restored with surgery. Typically a cataract will appear as an opacity in the lens of one eye or both. Cataracts can be caused by inherited diseases; trauma; or diabetes mellitus, which, in simple terms, is the failure of the pancreas to regulate the dog's blood sugar.

Progressive Retinal Atrophy (PRA) Two types of PRA affect dogs—generalized and central; Labs are affected by central PRA. In the disease, the rods in the retina deteriorate first causing a loss of night vision. Then the cones degenerate, causing total blindness. There is no treatment.

Entropion This malformation of the eyelid is a relatively common genetic condition among Labs. The eyelid is inverted or folded inward, causing a painful corneal ulceration. Surgical correction is needed for this condition.

INTERNAL DISEASES AND OTHER CONDITIONS

Tricuspid Valve Dysplasia (TVD) Some Labradors suffer from a genetically-based type of heart valve malformation that causes symptoms such as stunted growth, loud breathing, and a buildup of fluid in the abdomen, which eventually leads to congestive heart failure. Symptoms can be treated in the short-term. However, long-term prognosis for the disease is generally poor.

Gastric Dilation-Volvulus (GDV)

Commonly referred to as "bloat," GDV occurs when a stomach distends with gas and then *twists*, effectively cutting off the blood supply to the intestines and eventually the heart. When the stomach initially fills with gas, the expanding stomach makes it difficult for the dog to breathe. When the twist occurs, the dog is in terrible pain and quickly goes into shock. If it's not treated as a dire emergency, the dog will die.

Symptoms to be aware of:

- Distended stomach
- Heavy drooling
- Attempts to vomit, belch
- Difficulty breathing
- Restlessness
- Other signs of pain (rapid pulse, rapid heartbeat, weak pulse)

Definitive causes for GDV remain elusive. In 2014, the AKC Canine Health Foundation wrote a Request for Proposals for the Bloat Research Initiative, in order to create a more comprehensive understanding of bloat. The areas of research are focusing on the genetic risk variants in high-risk breeds (looking for genetic markers), if stress enhances susceptibility of dogs to bloat, if dogs that bloat have a defect in their GI nervous system, if perhaps dogs

that bloat have abnormally slow movement of food through their GI tract, and more.

Currently it is thought that stress plays a role in bloat; large breeds with deep chests are more prone to suffer this type of emergency, and dogs that gobble their food down could have more issues. To solve the latter issue, Lab owners can add large dog toys to the dog's food bowl and force the Lab to pick around the toys to eat his food.

Exercise-induced Collapse (EIC) This is an actual, inherited trait in the Labrador Retriever—for which there is a genetic test. Symptoms of the disease appear as a dog enters between five to twenty minutes of intense exercise, stress, or duress, and can include abnormal rocking, weaving gait; dragging the back legs while running; standing in a wide-legged stance; staggering, falling while running; front legs stiff when collapsed, or an inability to move the head while collapsed; and/or a high body temperature. Treatment of dogs with EIC include changes in activities, dietary changes, neutering, and possibly medications.

Hypothyroidism In addition to gaining weight, the Lab with hypothyroidism will show symptoms of lethargy, hair loss, and may have problems with recurrent infections or wounds that won't heal. Hypothyroidism can be treated successfully with medications for the lifetime of the pet.

CANCERS

According to some estimates, 50 percent of all dogs over the age of ten will develop some form of cancer. Of the many types of cancers, the two most common forms seen in dogs are malignant lymphomas (blood cancer) and mast cell tumors (tumors that cause allergic responses, gastric ulcers, and internal bleeding). These two types of cancer are also over-represented in the Labrador Retriever.

Although there is no known way to protect your Lab from cancer at this time, you can do your best to catch the early symptoms of cancer as quickly as possible. As with *any* disease, the sooner you can get a diagnosis, the faster your dog can begin receiving treatment, which will give your dog the greatest chance at a *possibility* of a better outcome.

So what should you be looking for? Every time you pat, rub, or brush your Lab, be aware of any unusual lumps or bumps. Is there a sore that isn't healing? That's something that should be checked *anyway* as it could be a sign of one of many disorders. When you trim your Lab's toenails, does he show unusual pain or sensitivity in his toes, paws, or higher up in his joints? Do you notice abnormal swelling in a limb or in an area of his body? Does he smell? A sudden change in odor that is not due to an obvious ear infection or anal gland issue (both of which are veterinary visits *anyway*) is cause for a visit to the veterinarian's office.

What are his eating habits like? Have you noticed any sudden changes in appetite or loss of appetite, weight loss, difficulty eating or swallowing? Be alert for changes in strength or exercise tolerance. An accident in the home with a formerly well housetrained Lab is a red flag that something is physically wrong and needs to be examined. Also, it is cause for concern if your Lab suddenly has difficulties with urinating or defecating.

And don't forget that "gut" feeling. You know your Lab better than anyone else. If you feel that something just isn't quite right, then it probably isn't. Note what you think is different about your Lab and don't discount any subtle changes in behaviors you observe.

Treatment options for cancers are continually evolving. Depending on the cancer, alternatives may range from chemotherapy, surgery, and radiation therapy, to medication and palliative care. If your Lab receives a cancer diagnosis, evaluate your options and make the treatment option that is best for you and your Lab.

Training Basics

Whether you know it or not, you now own one of the most amazing breeds to train in the dog world. The Labrador Retriever is the dog of choice for many in competitive performance dog sports, and he is a fantastic choice for the novice or first time dog owner.

Why is the Lab so trainable? There are many reasons. One, he is incredibly intelligent. Two, he picks up almost intuitively on what you are trying to teach him. This is in part because of his hunting background: He was bred to be very focused on his handler and look to his handler for instruction. That high level of focus can still be found in today's Lab at an amazingly young age. Many pups can be taught to *sit* as early as five weeks of age. And three, he *enjoys* training. Again, this is part of his close-working, hunting heritage—he was bred for centuries to work closely with his hunting partner. He *lives* to work all day with his owner. The Lab is most happy when he is learning new skills (being challenged mentally), working outside (exercise), and receiving praise and rewards from his favorite person.

The Lab is also a favorite among trainers because he is very forgiving of handler mistakes. This doesn't mean you should take advantage of his kind soul and abuse him with any negative or harsh training methods. Positive, reward-based training methods will work perfectly well with the Lab and are more enjoyable for everyone involved.

PRINCIPLES OF POSITIVE, REWARD-BASED TRAINING

The basic principles of positive, reward-based training are exactly as you would expect. The training is kept "positive," in that there are no physical or verbal corrections made to the dog. This means that in positive training, hands are used for patting, rubbing, and gently holding or shaping the dog into positions. Hands are not used (in the nega-

tive) to grab, slap, hit, yank, slam, or force a dog into a position. In positive training, the voice is used joyfully for encouragement, praise, and to let the dog know he is doing or has done something right, and later for commands. The voice is never raised (negatively) at the dog as a means to frighten, punish, terrorize, or otherwise serve as a severe and terrible correction when he has done something you didn't want him to do.

The reward part of this training comes as verbal and physical praise *from you.* Your Lab's ultimate reward will always be the reward that you personally give him. The training treats you give him as rewards are great in his early training and will help

immensely in shaping or creating the behaviors you want him to produce (more on this in a moment)—but remember, your Lab's ultimate reward is your physical and verbal praise.

USING TRAINING TREATS TO SHAPE BEHAVIORS

Food treats are excellent ways to shape behaviors quickly, easily, and without squashing a young pup's enthusiasm or getting into a huge wrestling match with an older, adolescent Lab that has some serious haunches and wriggle moves. If done correctly, using a tiny bit of food as a lure, a handler can teach a dog to *sit* and *down* without ever touching the pup.

When using a treat as a lure, there are just a few basic rules to follow.

Rule 1: Give the treat when the pup achieves something. This is important. The dog must make progress to earn a treat. For example, in the *down*, if the Lab is keeping his haunches on the floor and lowering his shoulders and head, that is progress. You can give him a treat. If he then follows the treat a little farther the next time so that he is *almost* lying all the way down on the floor, you can give him a treat. If the third time, he goes back to just lowering his shoulders and head, he doesn't get a treat. He doesn't get admonished either. You would reset him. Lure him back into a *sit* and then start the process of luring him into a *down* again.

Toys Work, Too!

You don't have to use only treats to shape behaviors. If you have a Lab that is toy-driven, a favorite ball or fetch toy can work equally as well as a lure.

Rule 2: Link the verbal command when the pup *completes* the behavior. Your Lab is very, very smart. So smart that the timing of *when* you link the voice command with the final behavior you want is important. If you say *"Sit"* as the Lab begins to sit and he fails to do so, you are teaching your Lab to squat. You want to say *"Sit"* just as your Lab nails the very last second of sitting. As your Lab begins to routinely rock back for the *sit*, then you can link the verbal command *"Sit"* earlier and earlier in the luring process until, eventually, you will ask for a *sit and not have to lure* at all—your Lab *sits*, and then is rewarded.

Important Note: Don't say a command multiple times. Again, your Lab is very smart. If you say *"Sit. Sit. Sit. SIT. SIT. SIT! SIT!! SIT!!!"* before your Lab actually sits, you have taught your Lab to *sit* after eight commands, not one. If saying *"Sit"* once does not have your Lab immediately hitting the floor with his bottom, then you need to lure him into a sit *without any anger or irritation.* When a dog "forgets" a command that means he isn't sure of himself, which in turn means that he needs more practice.

Rule 3: Make Every Practice, Perfect Practice There is a saying among musicians, "Practice doesn't make perfect but perfect practice does." It's the same with dog training. The more perfectly you can get your Lab to perform an exercise each and every time, the more precisely he will remember it, and the more exactly he will repeat it for you on command.

To get your Lab to perform the exercise as perfectly as possible before he even knows what the exercise is, you have to set up the situation so that it is almost impossible for him to fail. For example, use a treat as a lure to rock your standing pup into a *sit*, while gently holding his collar—this is setting him up to succeed at sitting.

But it goes even further than simply using a lure to shape the behavior. Perfect practice means that you need to be aware of three training factors: environment, distance, and time.

- Environment: When teaching a new command, begin training in a location with no distractions—a quiet indoor room with no other pets, children, or family members present. Once the dog is solid on the command (can perform the behavior ten times on voice command with no hesitation), then you move to a new environment or introduce a distraction *but* take a step back in your training of the behavior to lure the behavior the first time (to set the dog up for success.)

- Distance: Train a new behavior right next to or in front of the dog, depending on the behavior. Once the dog is solid on the command (see above), you may give the command one step away from the dog. Or, if the command is the *stay* command, you may give the command and then take one

step away and then step immediately back, building up distance over time.

- **Time:** Time is important in training in two ways. First, in a broad sense, time is important as it relates to the amount of time you spend training your Lab. Early on, you don't want to train longer than your pup's attention span, so puppy training

should be shorter sessions spread throughout the day. As the pup ages, you can move to a longer session once a day.

Second, time is also important in training as it relates to the length of time in which you ask a dog to "hold" or maintain a behavior. A good example is the *stay* command. Initially, ask the pup to *sit-*

stay for five seconds, give him praise, and release him. Then, when he is successful for five to six repetitions, increase the time to ten seconds, and so on.

With "perfect practice" or "setting a dog up for success" what you *don't* do is change more than one factor—environment, distance, or time—at the same moment. Change *one* factor in the exercise, keeping everything else the same. This makes it easier for the dog to learn what you want him to do.

TEACHING THE BASICS: *SIT, STAY, DOWN,* AND *COME*

When it comes to transforming a wild, unruly Lab puppy into a focused, enthusiastic, ready-to-learn-more companion, it often takes only four simple commands: *sit, stay, down,* and *come*. And don't feel that you have to wait until a spot opens up in a basic puppy training class to start training your Lab. *sit, stay, down,* and *come* are very simple behaviors that you can teach your Lab at home.

Training the *Sit*

Each behavior that is taught in this chapter will follow the pattern of shaping the behavior with a lure, rewarding the behavior, linking the behavior with a verbal command, and then practicing the behavior. Remember to only increase environment, distance, or time *one at a time* when making the exercise more difficult.

To train the *sit*, begin with these simple steps:

- **Shape the *Sit*:** Gently hold your pup's collar in one hand, and using the treat as a lure in the other hand, hold the treat right above the pup's nose and slowly pass it back across the Lab's nose toward his eyes and ears, forcing him to rock back on his haunches into a *sit*.
- **Reward the Behavior:** When his haunches *are on the ground* reward him with the treat. Tell him he's a good boy! You can also reward progress toward sitting until he finally reaches a full *sit*. Just be very careful not to link the verbal command at this time.
- **Link the Verbal Command, "*Sit!*":** When your puppy is successfully following the lure and virtually sitting the moment he sees you pull out the treat, *then* you can begin linking the verbal command, "*Sit!*"

When he's slow or hesitates...

If at any time your Lab looks hesitant or is doing an exercise really slowly, he is confused or uncertain. Take the exercise back one or two steps so that it is easier, back to a point where your pup is confident and can do the exercise really well. Practice here for a while and then begin to build back up again to a more difficult point.

with the action of sitting. Make sure you wait to say *"Sit!"* when you are sure he is going to sit. Reward him with the treat and praise.

- **Repeat & Increase Difficulty:** Repeat, treat, and praise. Back up the timing of when you say, *"Sit!"* until you are saying it earlier and earlier in the process of him sitting down. (This is an example of changing the variable of "time.") Treat and praise. Eventually, you will be able to say *"Sit!"* and your Lab will slam it to the floor.

When to Use the *Sit*

Use the *sit* every time your Lab puppy wants to receive pats: the recipient doesn't get knocked down, and the *sit* becomes a self-rewarding behavior for the Lab puppy (i.e., every time he sits, he gets patted! How great is that!) Use a *sit* before you put his food bowl down. Use a *sit* when opening the front door to keep a Lab *in* as guests arrive. Also, asking your Lab to sit periodically throughout the day is a great way to exercise leadership in a non-confrontational way.

Teaching the *Stay*

The *stay* can be taught in many different positions, such as the *sit-stay, down-stay, stand-stay, upside-down-stay,* okay, that last one is not an official one but you could teach a lazy Lab to do that one really well, too. Basically, the *stay* command is one that tells your Lab to remain in place *and* in position.

Because your Lab knows how to *sit,* you can work on the *sit-stay* first.

How Many Repetitions?

If your dog can repeat an exercise confidently eight out of ten times, you're ready to make the exercise a little harder.

- Shape the *sit-stay*: Put a leash on your Lab's collar. With your Lab on your left side, ask him to *"Sit."*
- Link the Verbal Command, *"Stay!"*: With your left hand, fingers down and the palm side of your hand facing directly in front of your pup's nose, move your hand from right-to-left in a short, brisk motion and stop in front of your dog's nose, say firmly, *"Stay!"* then stand up calmly. Count three seconds.
- Reward the *stay*: Calmly treat, praise, and reward your dog.
- Repeat and Increase Difficulty: Repeat linking the voice and hand signal to the idea of *stay* to the dog for at least ten solid repetitions. *Then* increase difficulty with either time (by adding ten seconds) or distance (taking one step to the right, holding it one second and stepping immediately back). Reward success, repeat until solid, and increase difficulty again. Eventually, you will want to be able to walk to the end of the leash, the end of two leashes tied together, to the other side of the room, watch a TV show, etc., but that will be months away. For now, take it in very, very small steps and remember if he is unsteady at *any time*, go back to where the Lab is steady and build his confidence back up. Note: when you introduce a new environment (go outside) *go back to the very beginning.* There are so many distractions outside that you will have to start from scratch. It won't take long to build back up but remember, set your Lab up for success!

When to Use the *Stay*

The *stay* command can help keep an exuberant Lab in a *sit* when greeting new people. A *down-stay* is an excellent calming command for a Lab when company is over or when you are eating dinner. You will not run out of possibilities for the *stay* command.

Teaching the *Down*

If there is a behavior that gives novices a little bit of a challenge, it will be the *down* command. Do not be disheartened. This happens to everyone. Keep trying. The Lab is a good student.

- Shape the *Down*: Holding your Lab's collar gently in one hand, and a treat in the other, show your Lab the treat and slowly bring the treat straight down between his paws to the floor and then slowly out along the floor, creating an "L" shape. This should bring his nose to the floor and then have him stretch down until his elbows hit the floor and he is lying down.

If your Lab pops his rump up, you might have better luck with this alternate training method. Sitting down, raise your knees up. Keeping your feet on the ground, so there is just enough room for your Lab to try to crawl through, take the treat in one hand and entice him as if you're trying to get him to crawl through your knees, but in actuality you're using your knees to get him in the *down* position.

- **Reward the Behavior:** When your Lab makes a complete *down*, reward him with the treat, your voice, and lots of pats! You can reward progression, too, particularly as the *down* can be a little more difficult to achieve than the *sit*. However, be sure not to link the voice command just yet.
- **Link the Verbal Command, "Down!":** Only when the Lab consistently makes a full and complete *down* with the lure, start linking the voice command with the behavior. You will want to say, *"Down!"* as

he is in the final movement of completing the *down*.

- **Repeat Until Solid:** Continue linking the verbal command with the *down* at the completion of the final movement. When your Lab is steady with this, back up the verbal command a little at a time until your Lab is easily going into a *down* at the beginning of the behavior. Always remember to reward the behavior with praise and treats. When your Lab knows the behavior very well, always reward with your voice and less frequently with treats.

When to Use the *Down*

The *down* can help settle an extremely excited Lab, or control a Lab while preparing dinner or serving a meal. The *down* position also makes it physically difficult (but not impossible) to bark, so if you are trying to control excessive barking, this is a good command to teach. The *down* is a submissive position, so use this behavior periodically to continue to strengthen your leadership position in a non-confrontational way.

Teaching the *Come*

The *come* command or "recall" is perhaps the most important command you will ever teach your Lab. In canine sports, the command is used routinely. If your Lab is a pet, *come* is a command you practice religiously, with hopes that if you are in a critical situation, your Lab will respond immediately.

- **Shape the *Come*:** Remember: Shape this behavior so that it is virtually impossible for your Lab to fail. You want him to succeed every time. There are many ways

to train this behavior. You are not limited to one training method! For this method, clip the leash on your Lab's collar, keeping the leash slack. Start walking or trotting backward. Get your Lab's attention by saying his name or "puppy, puppy, puppy," or something that sounds fun, so he starts trotting or galloping toward you playfully.

• Reward the Behavior: While the puppy is moving toward you, reward him with verbal praise. He is being a *good* boy. He is coming toward you and this is what you want. When he comes to you, scoop him up and give him rubs and play the game some more. Treats are great rewards right as he comes in for his big finish, as are toys.

• Link the Verbal Command, *"Come!"*: This is an easy behavior to link a verbal command to, but you will need to watch your timing. Say *"Come!"* right as your Lab runs into your legs. This is setting your pup up to succeed.

• Repeat and Increase Difficulty: Continue to play the recall training as a game, on leash, and link the verbal command right as your Lab finishes. To increase the difficulty, start backing up the timing of the command, *"Come!"* so that it is earlier and earlier in the timing of your Lab's run toward you. When he's mastered this, with your Lab still on leash, put him in a *sit-stay*, take three steps out in front of him, turn around and face him, give him the recall command *"Come!"* and immediately start running backward again as you did when you first started training the recall and verbally encouraging him. Tell him how good he is when he comes to you! Reward, praise, treat! Repeat and you know the drill … work until he's solid and then make it a little harder.

DON'T DRAG ME! *WALK NICELY*

If you teach your Lab to *walk nicely* on a leash at an early age, you will rarely have an issue as he grows older. When working with a little puppy, use the lightest leash possible. A heavy, full-size brass clip swinging into the face of a puppy can be a bit off-putting, so find a leash made for a dog up to 25 pounds (11 kg) and realize you're going to replace it with a sturdier one in a few weeks.

Clip the leash to the puppy's collar and immediately start walking and talking. Your goal is to keep your puppy's attention on you. You want to be the most interesting thing around. Give him treats if he's walking on a loose leash and staying around you. What a good boy! You are rewarding good behavior with your voice and with treats. Keep a favorite toy with you and squeak it occasionally to get his attention and then give it to him as a reward. Trade a treat for the toy, pocket the toy, and continue walking.

If he starts to veer left, walk right and say his name, encouraging him to follow. (Be sure not to say *"C'mon"* or *"Come"* as that is a different command.) When he follows, reward him with praise, an excited voice, pats, a little run or pep to your step, etc., and then straighten out your walk and continue on your way. Do the same if he veers right—walk left. If he rushes forward, start walking backward and encourage him to turn around. The moment he does, take off running and reward him. Then resume walking in the correct direction. Keep it fun and exciting!

The key is to keep mixing it up whenever the Lab strays, so that *you* remain the most interesting object on the walk. Or, if he gets distracted, his focus is easily returned to you by just saying his name or a few quick words.

WORKING WITH OLDER, PULLING LABS

Maybe you didn't exactly work on leash training your puppy when he was young, or maybe you adopted an older Lab. Whatever the reason, now your Lab is 60 pounds of enthusiastic, pulling, dragging, galloping mess on a leash. You can still work with the technique described above but with a regular leash, of course. You will want to begin training in an area with few distractions before you go into the great outdoors, too.

So, what do you do for walks in the meantime? A few immediate solutions are available.

- **Head halter:** This halter is a kind solution to dogs that pull hard and is based on the principle that when the dog pulls with a head halter, it will pull the dog right around to face you. The dog quickly learns that pulling does not achieve forward motion.
- **No-pull harness:** There are two types of no-pull harnesses. One type works similarly to the head halter in that the leash attaches to a ring at the center of the dog's chest.

When the dog pulls, he pulls himself around to face you and learns that pulling does not achieve a forward motion. The other type of no-pull harness applies pressure around the dog's chest and leg area, restraining the dog from pulling.

Note that all of these temporary heavy-pulling solutions require proper fitting, and that they aren't permanent solutions. The best solution is continuing to work on your Lab's leash training until he learns to walk on a loose leash. Until that point, there's no reason to risk shoulder surgery from a sudden lurch or broken ribs from going "superman" with an uncontrollable Lab. Enjoy walking your Lab now and continue working on his skills.

If you've purchased your pup from a quality breeder, he will be coming home with a great start on his socialization skills. Because the potential for his great temperament is genetic, and the ability to bring out (or reverse) that potential is environmental, your puppy will have had eight weeks of ideal exposures to developing a terrific, people, and dog-friendly temperament.

Now that the pup is home, it's your turn to continue the good work.

Making Introductions

The great thing about socialization is that it is "self-rewarding" for the Lab puppy that likes to receive attention. Every time the puppy receives pats for wiggling and kissing people, he has effectively been rewarded for being friendly. He learns very quickly that no one is a stranger. So, on-leash social-ization becomes very easy with a friendly, calm puppy.

The Friendly, Calm Puppy

- Go on a walk.
- "May my puppy say hello?"
- Allow your puppy *on a loose leash* to walk up to the person to say hello.
- Praise your puppy for saying hello.

The Energetic, Bold Puppy

You know this puppy: the one that sees someone and starts *dragging* you to say hello and knocks the child over or jumps up to kiss the person in the face. Not good. For the energetic Lab, and this will be 90 percent of puppy owners, use this method:

- Put the Lab in a *sit-stay*.
- Ask the person if they would like to offer your Lab a treat.
- Give the child/person the treat and explain that your Lab has to stay very still to earn the treat and only his tail can move very fast.
- Praise your Lab softly for being so good and thank the child/person for helping you train your Lab.

Your Lab will eventually learn to *sit* for attention from strangers, and you can continue socializing him without worrying that he will knock anyone down.

The Timid, Reticent Lab

On rare occasions, you may find you have a Lab that is lacking in confidence. *Do not force this Lab to make introductions.* The approach to socializing the timid puppy is different.

Allow the Lab puppy to make the approach. If you see *any* signs of fear (see "Body Language to Watch" below) from the puppy, call the puppy back to you and tell him how good he is for coming to you. Allow the puppy to watch from a greater distance or until he shows more interest in meeting the person.

- Have a person you know toss a treat half-way to the puppy so he can approach the person and yet still remain in his comfort zone.
- Have the person next offer the puppy treats from an open palm, but not attempt to pat the puppy.
- When the pup comes up to the stranger to receive pats, make sure the stranger knows *not to pat the pup on the top of the head* but rather scratch the pup under the chin.
- Try to build as many positive experiences as possible, and avoid putting your Lab in any situations that could be frightening.

Body Language to Watch
Signs of Fear

- Head lowers, eyes looking up
- Eyes look away, trying not to make contact
- Ears pulled back and flat against neck
- Nervous panting
- Body is trembling or shaking; crouching; tries to hide behind you; tries to run away
- Submissive urination
- Tucked tail; may be wagging and tucked
- Crying, whimpering, barking, or silent

Activities for the Lab

All Labs can benefit from being active in sports, whether that sport is a performance event, a non-competitive activity, or the certification of being a well-trained companion dog.

The key to participation in many of these sporting events is registration with the American Kennel Club (AKC). Once your Lab is registered, if you want to participate in an event that is sponsored by another governing body or registry, you will usually be able to do so.

With the AKC, there are three different levels of registration.

FULL REGISTRATION

This certificate is white with a purple border and allows the Lab to compete in all AKC events. Also, if the dog is bred, its puppies can be registered. A quality breeder will only provide the form for a full registration if he or she believes the puppy has exceptional potential in either the conformation ring or field. This puppy will come with a detailed contract as to what you can and can't do with him.

LIMITED REGISTRATION

This certificate is white with an orange border and makes the Lab ineligible to be shown in the conformation ring. If the Lab is bred, its puppies cannot be registered. Typically, the breeder will require you to show proof of spay/neuter before you receive your puppy's Limited Registration forms from the breeder. A Limited Registration allows the Lab to participate in all AKC events except conformation.

PUREBRED ALTERNATIVE LISTING (PAL)

If you do not have any registration papers for your purebred Lab puppy, or perhaps you adopted a Lab, you can apply for a PAL that will enable you to compete in all AKC

performance events open to Labs, except conformation and field trials. To apply for a PAL, the dog must appear to be a purebred Lab, six months or older, spayed or neutered, and not registered as another breed. The application requires two photos of the dog (with specific directions on how to take these photos), and a processing fee.

Once your Lab has his registration, you can start working on adding letters after his name! Or just have fun. Or both!

THE OH-SO-GOOD LAB

A great place to start your Lab is with the AKC's S.T.A.R. Puppy program, which progresses into the Good Citizen program.

- **S.T.A.R. Puppy:** This program is a basic puppy training class with the added benefit of helping owners learn how to best communicate with their dogs. The class goes a bit further than basic training and includes practical skills and puppy-raising troubleshooting. A test is given at the end of a six week class.
- **Canine Good Citizen (CGC):** The CGC is a ten-step test that is designed to test dogs on their manners at home and in the community, as well as responsible pet ownership. Test items include such things as "Sitting politely for petting" and "Walking through a crowd." The CGC is an AKC title

and once a registered or PAL Lab passes the test, the title will appear on his record.

- **Community Canine (CGCA):** The AKC Community Canine is the Advanced CGC title. As with the CGC, the CGCA has a ten-step test of skills to test the dog on his manners; however, these are all done in environments such as pet stores, dog shows, or community settings, in order to be as realistic as possible. The CGCA is also an AKC title and appears on the dog's record.

THE PERFORMANCE LAB

Agility

Agility is one of the fastest growing sports in the dog world. In an agility trial, the handler directs the Lab through a series or course of obstacles, such as tunnels, teeter-totters, ramps, jumps, and weave poles. Many dog owners begin by taking agility classes to teach their dogs something new and wind up having so much fun that they pick up agility as a sport. There are several types of classes offered at agility trials. Each tests different skill sets, such as speed, accuracy, timing, distance handling, fastest time, strategy, etc., while using different obstacles. Additionally, there are three levels of difficulty within AKC agility: Novice, Open, Excellent/Master. And this is just AKC Agility.

Other organizations that hold agility events include: Canine Performance Events, Inc. (CPE); North American Dog Agility Council (NADAC); United Kennel Club (UKC);

and United States Dog Agility Association (USDAA). The classes and levels will vary within each organization, with some similarities. Those who compete in agility will make themselves familiar with the rules between the different competitions and will be able to compete in all once registered.

DockDogs

This is considered the "World's Premier Canine Aquatics Competition" and is billed as the event where anybody with any dog can have fun. Labs tend to dominate in this sport as it combines a love of retrieving, jumping off a dock, and water. DockDogs has three individual events: Big Air, Speed Retrieve, and Extreme Vertical—and the combined event,

Iron Dog, which is similar to a triathlon in that the dog competes in all three of DockDogs events for a combined high score.

Big Air records the dog that jumps the farthest distance off the dock to retrieve a fetch toy. Speed Retrieve times how long it takes a dog to retrieve a fetch toy suspended at the end of the water. And Extreme Vertical is the canine equivalent of a high jump for dogs in which the dog jumps off the dock to grab a bumper toy suspended out 8 ft (2.4 m) from the end of the dock over the water and 4 ft, 6 in (1.2 m, 15 cm) above the water. The bumper is raised 2 in (5 cm) every round as competition progresses.

DockDogs uses the same types of starting, finish, measuring, and capture equipment as that used in Olympic events, so rest assured there will be no questions as to finish times or distances achieved. Events are held across the country, and training clubs are being added in areas where the sport is particularly popular.

The UKC also holds a form of dock jumping sport that Labs can participate in.

Obedience

Obedience is a titled event and is one of the AKC's oldest canine sports, dating back to the 1930s. Many of the preliminaries to exercises required to pass the Novice level in Obedience are routinely taught in basic puppy classes: *sit, stay, down, come,* and *walk nicely.*

In the Novice level, exercises include Heel on Leash, in which the dog is required to walk precisely at the handler's left side, whether the handler speeds up to a trot or slows down to a slow walk or turns right or turns left or makes a U-turn. Whenever the handler stops, the dog quickly and neatly *sits.* When the handler moves forward, the dog immediately and crisply moves forward with the handler and with no lag. The handler and dog must also show their heeling prowess by navigating around two people in a figure eight.

In addition to Heel on Leash and Figure Eight, the Novice level of Obedience requires: Heel Free (no leash!), Stand for Examination (*Stand-Stay*), Recall, Long Sit (off-leash, in the group class, one minute across ring from the handler), Long Down (off-leash, in group class, three minutes across ring from the handler).

The three levels of Obedience are Novice, Open, and Utility. The UKC also offers Obedience titles.

Rally

Rally is considered a companion sport to AKC Obedience. A rally course has ten to twenty stations (depending on the skill level). At each station, the dog is required to perform a skill. A skill may be "change pace," "turn 360 degrees," "about U-turn," or "sit-stay."

You are allowed to talk to your dog, encourage him, and be enthusiastic. Scoring is not as rigorous as in formal obedience and heeling position is not required to be quite as perfect. The levels in rally are: Novice, Advanced, and Excellent.

The Association of Pet Dog Trainers (APDT) also offers Rally as a sport for dogs.

Tracking

The AKC offers four different titles in tracking: Tracking Dog (TD), Tracking Dog Urban (TDU), Tracking Dog Excellent (TDX), and Variable Surface Tracking (VST). The tracking dog titles of TD and TDU are pass/fail and one or the other must be earned before competing for the TDX. If a dog with a TDX is able to earn a VST, he is awarded a Champion Tracker (CT) title and is considered to be among the elite of tracking dogs.

Tracking is a very popular sport in which a tracklayer (person) lays a path and drops articles along the path. The dog, in a tracking harness and on a 20 to 40 ft (6 m to 12 m) tracking line, must first find the start of the track and then without the aid of the handler, follow the track and indicate the articles along the track to the handler. The judges follow the handler and dog along the way to determine if the dog is working, if the dog loses the track and cannot find the track, if the dog misses an article, etc.

THE GUN DOG

Without a doubt, working with your Lab and doing what comes naturally to him can be a profoundly rewarding activity for both you and your pup. Some Labs will have intense drives, others less so, but virtually all Labs will have *some* hunting drives. If you want to see how far your Lab can go, this is where you should start.

Working Certificate Program

This program was started by the Labrador Retriever Club, Inc. (LRC) in 1931 and remains as a great test for novice owners today who want to see if their Lab has natural retrieving instincts. The program has two levels, the Working Certificate (WC) and the Working Certificate Excellent (WCX). The best way to get prepared for the WC is to contact your local Labrador Retriever club to find a good training

club in your area. To pass the WC, the Lab must be able to do the following:
- not be gun-shy
- retrieve a shot bird 50 yards on land in light cover
- successfully retrieve two ducks from water, one right after the other
- return the birds to the handler

Hunt Tests

The AKC holds non-competitive, titling hunt tests for retrievers. The titles are: Junior Hunter (JH), Senior Hunter (SH), and Master Hunter (MH). In order to title, a Lab must receive three qualifying scores on three separate tests. The Junior Hunter test includes single marked retrieves on land and water. The marked retrieve is a retrieve in which the Lab sits next to the handler, sees the bird in flight, a gunner (not the handler) takes the actual shot, the dog sees the trajectory of the fall, the handler then sends the Lab out to retrieve the bird and recalls the dog, to which the dog is to return the bird within a reasonable distance to the handler. The Lab is allowed to be lightly restrained at the line.

The Senior level is more difficult than the Junior level, and by the time the Lab has reached the Master level, he is an exceptional hunting dog. In addition to the AKC, the Hunting Retriever Club, a division of the UKC, and the North American Hunting Retriever Association (NAHRA), offer variations of hunt tests, too.

Field Trials

Retriever field trials were developed back in the late 1920s, specifically to evaluate the

performance of hunting retrievers. Nearly one hundred years later, retriever field trials are just as competitive—in fact, even more so. The sport began with marked retrieves and blinds (retrieves in which the Lab doesn't see the trajectory of the shot bird and is directed by the handler) that were rarely farther than 100 yards (91 m) away. Today, to determine winners in a field of finalists in a field trial, winning field trial Labs have to routinely make *multiple* marked retrieves in excess of

250 yards (228 m) and/or blind retrieves up to 300 yards (274 m) or more.

Amateurs and professionals alike compete in field trials, but keep in mind that the amateurs who are involved are exceptionally experienced handlers and trainers and often their dogs are professionally trained. If you think you'd like to get involved in field trials, one of the best ways to get started is to attend a field trial and talk to those who are in attendance.

Information

USEFUL ADDRESSES AND CONTACTS

Organizations

American Kennel Club (AKC)
5580 Centerview Drive
Raleigh, NC 27606-3390
919-233-9767
www.akc.org

Canadian Kennel Club
200 Ronson Drive, Suite 400
Etobicoke, Ontario CANADA
M9W 5Z9
416-675-5511
www.ckc.ca

The Kennel Club (United Kingdom)
1-5 Clarges Street
Piccadilly, London W1J 8AB
0844 463 3980
www.the-kennel-club.org.uk

United Kennel Club (UKC)
100 East Kilgore Road
Kalamazoo, Michigan 49002-5584
269-343-9020
www.ukcdogs.com

Labrador Retriever Club, Inc. (AKC)
www.thelabradorclub.com
inquiry@thelabradorclub.com

National Labrador Retriever Club (FCI)
www.nationallabradorretrieverclub.com

Health/Veterinary Information
American Veterinary Medical Association
1931 North Meacham Road, Suite 100
Schaumburg, IL 60173-4360
(800) 248-2862
www.avma.org
avmainfo@avma.org

ACTIVITIES

Agility

American Kennel Club (AKC)
See listing under "Organizations"

Canine Performance Events, Inc. (CPE)
P.O. Box 805
South Lyon, MI 48178
www.k9cpe.com

North American Dog Agility Council (NADAC)
P.O. Box 1206
Colbert, OK 74733
www.nadac.com
info@nadac.com

United Kennel Club (UKC)
See listing under "Organizations"

United States Dog Agility Association (USDAA)
P.O. Box 850995
Richardson, Texas 75085
(972) 487-2200
www.usdaa.com

Canine Good Citizen
See "American Kennel Club" listing

Conformation
See "American Kennel Club" listing
See "United Kennel Club" listing

Dock Jumping
DockDogs
www.dockdogs.com
See "United Kennel Club" listing

Field Trials/Hunt Tests
See "American Kennel Club" listing
See "United Kennel Club" listing

Obedience
See "American Kennel Club" listing
See "United Kennel Club" listing

Rally
See "American Kennel Club" listing
Association of Pet Dog Trainers (APDT)
101 North Main Street, Suite 610
Greenville, SC 29601
1-800-PET-DOGS (1-800-738-3647)
www.apdt.com

Tracking
See "American Kennel Club" listing

BOOKS

Activities
Agility: Leach, Laurie. *The Beginner's Guide to Dog Agility*. Neptune, New Jersey: TFH, Inc., 2006.

Canine Good Citizen: Volhard, Jack, and Wendy Volhard. *The Canine Good Citizen: Every Dog Can Be One*, 2nd Edition. New York: John Wiley & Sons, Inc., 1997.

Obedience: Donaldson, Jean. *Train Your Dog Like a Pro*. New York: Howell Book House, 2010.

Rally: Eldredge, Debra. *The Ultimate Guide to Rally-O: Rules, Strategies, and Skills for Successful Rally Obedience Competition*. Neptune, New Jersey: TFH, Inc., 2011.

Tracking: Krause, Carolyn. *Try Tracking! The Puppy Tracking Primer*. Wenatchee, WA: Dogwise Publishing, 2005.

Behavior/Training
General Dog Behavior: Aloff, Brenda. *Canine Body Language, A Photographic Guide*. Wenatchee, WA: Dogwise Publishing, 2005.

Housetraining: Palika, Liz. *The Pocket Idiot's Guide to Housetraining Your Dog*. New York: Penguin Group (USA), 2007.

Socializing with Dogs: Bennett, Robin, and Susan Briggs. *Off-leash Dog Play: A Complete Guide to Safety and Fun*. Woodbridge, VA: C&R Publishing, LLC, 2008.

Socializing with People: Long, Lorie. *A Dog Who's Always Welcome: Assistance and Therapy Dog Trainers Teach You How to Socialize and Train Your Companion Dog*. New York: John Wiley & Sons, Inc., 2008.

Important Note

This pet owner's manual tells the reader how to buy or adopt, and care for, a Labrador Retriever. The author and publisher consider it important to point out that the advice given in the book is meant primarily for normally developed dogs of excellent physical health and sound temperament.

Anyone who acquires a fully-grown dog should be aware that the animal has already formed its basic impressions of human beings. The new owner should watch the animal carefully, including its behavior toward humans, and, whenever possible, should meet the previous owner.

Caution is further advised in the association of children with dogs, in meeting with other dogs, and in exercising the dog without a leash.

Even well-behaved and carefully supervised dogs sometimes do damage to someone else's property or cause accidents. It is therefore in the owner's interest to be adequately insured against such eventualities, and we strongly urge all dog owners to purchase a liability policy that covers their dog.

Index

About the Author

Joan Hustace Walker is the author of more than 20 pet books including *Barron's Dog Bible: Labrador Retrievers*. She has written hundreds of feature articles, has photographed hundreds of published images, and has received more than 30 national and international nominations and awards for her vast body of work.

Cover Photos

Shutterstock: front cover: left: Eric Isselee; top right: DragoNika; middle right: Janelle Lugge; bottom right: Rita Kochmarjova; back cover: otsphoto; inside front cover: Capture Light; inside back cover: Vivienstock

Photo Credits

Deby Andrus Photography: page 95
Fotolia: Andres Rodriguez: pages 42, 52; Anna Auerbach: page 16; Conny Hagen: page 70; dazb75: page 82; Dogs: page 26; DragoNika: page 4; La India Piaroa: page 56; Rita Kochmarjova: page 86; Viorel Sima: page 29; WavebreakMediaMicro: page 51; yarvet: page 93; Zach Cunningham: page 8, 89; Željko Radojko: page 55
iStock: AlexRaths: page 69; AngiePhotos: page 73; happyborder: page 83; s5iztok: page 84; tderden: page 44
Shutterstock: ARTSILENSE: page 9; Baevskiy Dmitry: page 10; cynoclub: pages 47, 68; Dagmar Hijmans: page 34; dezi: pages 7, 33, 53, 66; Dora Zett: page 25; DragoNika: pages 2, 11, 14, 60; Eric Isselee: pages 3, 13, 15, 19, 39, 41, 64, 75; Hannamariah: page 23; iko: pages 48, 50; Iuliia Bondarenko: page 31; Ivan Mladenov: page 59; Jagodka: page 20, 32; James E. Knopf: page 85; Janelle Lugge: page 38; Jari Hindstroem: page 40; Jaromir Chalabala: pages 46, 62; Kirk Geisler: pages 5, 12; markos86: page 72, 79; Martin Maun: page 77; Nina Buday: page 80; otsphoto: pages 6, 24, 28, 30, 57, 67; paolo airenti: page 17; rebeccaashworth: pages 22, 88; Rita Kochmarjova: page 21; Sam Strickler: page 63; Stephanie Zieber: page 74; Tatiana Gass: page 65; Vivienstock: pages 27, 43; Viorel Sima: pages 35, 76, 90
Joan Hustace Walker: pages 18, 36

Dedication

This book is dedicated to the memory of Hudson Steele, and to his faithful Lab, Troy, who continues to provide love and comfort to the Steele family until he is called to join his boy.

A Note on Pronouns

Many dog lovers feel that the pronoun "it" is not appropriate when referring to a beloved pet. For this reason, Labrador Retrievers are referred to as "he" throughout this book, unless the topic specifically relates to female dogs. No gender bias is intended by this writing style.

© Copyright 2015 by Barron's Educational Series, Inc.

All rights reserved.
No part of this book may be reproduced or distributed in any form, or by any other means without the written permission of the copyright owner.

All inquiries should be addressed to:
Barron's Educational Series, Inc.
250 Wireless Boulevard
Hauppauge, NY 11788
www.barronseduc.com

ISBN: 978-1-4380-0487-7
Library of Congress Control Number: 2014957242

Printed in China
9 8 7 6 5 4 3 2 1